THE Prayer Shawl COMPANION

38 knitted designs to embrace inspire & celebrate life

JANET BRISTOW & VICTORIA A. COLE-GALO

Photographs by Tom Hopkins

The Taunton Press

Text © 2008 by Janet Bristow and
Victoria A. Cole-Galo
Photographs © 2008 by Tom Hopkins
Photography
Illustrations © 2008 by Christine Erikson
The Taunton Press, Inc.

The Taunton Press, Inc.,
63 South Main Street, PO Box 5506, Newtown,
CT 06470-5506
e-mail: tp@taunton.com

Editor: Erica Sanders-Foege
Copy editor: Candace B. Levy
Indexer: Lynne Lipkind
Jacket/Cover design: Kimberly Adis
Interior design: Kimberly Adis
Layout: Kimberly Adis
Illustrator: Christine Erikson
Photographer: Tom Hopkins Photography,
Wendi Mijal

Library of Congress Cataloging-in-Publication
Data
Bristow, Janet.
  The prayer shawl companion : 38 knitted
designs to embrace, inspire, and celebrate life
/ Janet Bristow and Victoria A. Cole-Galo.
     p. cm.
  Includes bibliographical references and index.
  ISBN 978-1-60085-003-5 (alk. paper)
  1. Knitting--Patterns. 2. Shawls. 3. Religion in
art. I. Cole-Galo, Victoria A. II. Title.
  TT825.B74 2008
  746.43'2041--dc22

  2008010202

Printed in China
10 9 8 7 6 5 4 3 2 1

The following manufacturers/names
appearing in *The Prayer Shawl Companion* are
trademarks: Acrilan®, Bernat®, Caron® Perfect
Match®, Caron® Simply Soft®, Caron® Wintuk®,
Jo-Ann™ Sensations™, Knit a Shrug—Give a
Hug™, Lion Brand® Jiffy®, Natural Focus™,
Patons®, Red Heart® Soft Yarn™, Red Heart®
Super Saver®, Red Heart® Symphony®

DEDICATION

This book is dedicated to all the

prayer shawl makers across the

country and around the world who,

with open hearts and hands,

pray shawls into being, giving them

to others as a gesture of compassion

and peace.

ACKNOWLEDGMENTS

Thanks to Taunton Press for giving us this wonderful opportunity and to the team that made this book happen. We are grateful that editor Erica Sanders-Foege patiently took us under her wing, leading us through the world of publishing. With impressive knowledge of the language of knitting and techniques, writer Betty Christiansen handled the material with sensitivity and care. We both are happy to call these women friends.

Thanks to all those who took the time to send us their beautiful patterns, shawls, touching stories, and prayers. Without you, this book would not be. To our mentor and friend, Miriam Therese Winter, our deepest thanks for gifting us with wisdom and encouragement.

Much appreciation to photographer Tom Hopkins whose outstanding work brought out the unique beauty of each shawl, and for the advice of Robert Izard, a champion of the Prayer Shawl Ministry.

We are grateful for the help of shawl makers and pattern testers Kathy Andreoli, Sherrie Czechowicz, Jane Gallagher, Rosann Guzauckas, Liz Hines, and Barbara Meany. Thanks also to the yarn companies for providing us with exquisite yarn.

From Janet: Thank you to my husband, Matt, and daughters, Beth and Amanda, whose love and encouragement have been the guiding light that frees me to follow my bliss. Thanks to my parents and grandparents for fostering pride in all things homemade and to my extended family and friends for their loving support.

From Vicky: All my love and gratitude to my husband, Zeke, and our sons, Jonathan and Nicholas, and to my parents—Gladys and Fran—mother-in-law Rita, brothers, and sisters-in-law. Thank you family and friends for your support, unconditional love, and bountiful blessings. Your spirit and gifts continue to enrich my life.

And last, but most important, we are humbled, honored, and grateful to our Creator, in whose hands this ministry lies.

Contents

FOREWORD

Some of life's most meaningful movements have the simplest beginnings. Who could have guessed that the gift of a shawl to one whose heart was broken would start a chain reaction felt around the world? It happened because this particular shawl and all that followed are genuine gifts of love. Spiraling out from Divine Love, who first knit *us* into being in the wombs of those who loved us, this creative endeavor replicates acts of loving kindness from that source of love within. Blessed are those who bring to birth new beginnings in another, thereby building a surrogate family of strangers becoming friends.

As our world unravels bit by bit in various ways, countless circles of compassion are knitting it back together again, one stitch at a time. Shawl recipients especially will see more clearly that there is hope for tomorrow, that no one is ever completely alone, that someone out there cares enough to reach out and welcome in. Let us pause to pray together as we prepare to enjoy this book.

O Love Divine,
Giver and Gift,
We thank You for the many times
You take the tangled threads of our lives
And create a thing of beauty.
Help us to do the same for others
Here, or near, or worlds away,
Symbolically, yet tangibly,
Through the gift of our hearts and hands.
Infuse this shawl with a blessing
That will always be present,
Always be felt
As comforting, all-encompassing love
Proportionate to one's need.
We send sustaining strength this day
To those who are crushed in spirit,
Wherever they may be.
May blessings abound
To and through
All who are knit together
In this ministry of love.
Amen.

—MIRIAM THERESE WINTER
Medical Mission Sister; author; singer; professor of liturgy, worship, and spirituality; and founder and director of the Women's Leadership Institute at Hartford Seminary in Connecticut.

PREFACE

When you think of a prayer shawl, what comes to mind? Is it the tallis, the fringed, four-cornered shawl worn by Jewish men and some women during services? Or is it the *hajib*, a prayer shawl from the Islamic tradition that modestly covers a woman from her head to her waist? For many knitters in America, the term *prayer shawl* brings another image to mind: A shawl that is lovingly hand knit or crocheted out of a soft, comforting yarn, blessed by the one who has made it, and wrapped around the shoulders of someone who needs the sort of comfort only the love and generosity of a caring friend can provide. We offer the prayer shawls in this book—as well as the stories, prayers, and blessings that accompany them—for your inspiration. And like most inspirations, there's a story behind ours.

The story of the Prayer Shawl Ministry is a journey that began in May 1997, when we graduated from the Women's Leadership Institute (WLI) at the Hartford Seminary in Hartford, Connecticut. Through it, we were able to connect with a broader, more inclusive, less gender-specific image of the Divine and with ourselves as women who minister to everyone in our lives. Free to seek the Divine in a safe environment, we had profound and blessed experiences of prayer and God's presence.

One such experience occurred when a member of our class asked us to pray with her for her husband, who was ill. As she wrapped herself in the brightly colored shawl she was wearing, we laid our hands on her and joined our prayers to hers, knowing that every time she wore her mantle, newly blessed by our prayers for the two of them, she would feel our love and support. The next time we saw the shawl, it was the altar cloth at her husband's funeral service. Its presence was powerful to us, knowing what it symbolized and that it would continue to be her source of solace and prayer. Without this experience, the ministry might not have happened.

Both of us were drawn to that shawl image, having seen firsthand the comfort a shawl can bring. It seemed to be the perfect metaphor for what we had experienced at the WLI and symbolic of the comforting, motherly, unconditionally loving God we had come to know. Vicky, who years before had experienced the comfort of a shawl in a period of distress, happened to be knitting at the time. Through prayer and meditation, she created the original knit three, purl three prayer shawl pattern. The pattern is a variation of the Seed Stitch (symbolic of "planting" our prayers) expanded to include the number three, which is symbolically significant in many cultures and religions.

As we prayerfully began to knit, the ritual of shawl making became a grounding influence in our everyday lives. The steady knit three, purl three rhythm became a soothing mantra, enabling us to focus beyond the process of knitting to the words spoken in our hearts to our God. Slowly, the Prayer Shawl Ministry began to knit itself within us. And, like butterflies emerging from their cocoons, the shawls unfolded from countless skeins of yarn.

As things progressed, we realized that our handwork was becoming our spiritual practice. It felt different from other work we did because we entered into the process through intention, meditation, and prayer. Our craft evolved into a new realm that was based in our spirituality as women.

Encouraged by our new awareness, we were eager to give gifts of shawls to family members and friends. The circle expanded as we heard of others in need of comfort. Sometimes, even when we thought we knew for whom the shawl was being made, the wrap would find its way to someone else, as we were serendipitously led into other people's lives. That's when we realized that we were being guided by God's Spirit.

Hand to Hand and Heart to Heart

As we gave the shawls away, others wanted to knit and give away shawls, too. Everyone, it seemed, knew someone who could benefit from receiving a shawl. Women, children, and men passed them on, person to person, hand to hand, and heart to heart. We began to see the potential that giving and receiving a shawl has in opening the doors of communication, reinforcing relationships, and inviting understanding and healing. For example, the gift of a shawl was a catalyst for a woman newly diagnosed with cancer to open up to her husband and talk about her fears. It enabled a man to finally grieve the demise of his marriage. It helped a grandmother teach her grandchild the prayers of her childhood, each wrapped in their own prayer shawl.

People were making shawls and mailing them to other parts of the state and around the country. Articles were published in journals and newspapers, from our own *Hartford Courant* to a paper in Johannesburg, South Africa. The response was overwhelming, and we realized that something big was happening, something beyond ourselves. That led us to create a website, www.shawlministry.com, which we like to think of as our e-book and as a wonderful example of how spirituality, craft, and technology can work together to reach and connect so many people.

Soon, people wanted to establish their own Prayer Shawl Ministry groups. To meet their needs, we started traveling to present Prayer Shawl Ministry workshops and retreats. Because being inclusive is important to us, we encouraged host groups to invite all faith communities and secular groups from their area to attend.

This book is a result of our ministry's growth. All of the patterns were kindly donated. Collected here are patterns by professional designers and by knitters from Prayer Shawl Ministries around the globe. Along with the patterns, you'll find stories that have been shared with us and what we call *blessings*, or contemplative words, to knit by. So there's much to fuel you on your prayer shawl knitting journey!

Upon reflection, we think the reason this ministry reaches so many people is that its guiding force is spirit led. We were eager and open to inspiration, ready to take the next step in our life journeys.

Welcome! May you be blessed threefold.
—*Janet Bristow and Victoria A. Cole-Galo*

BEGINNING PRAYERFULLY

PRAYER SHAWLS BECOME TANGIBLE SYMBOLS OF LOVE WHEN words can't be found to adequately express one's feelings. They can be warm hugs of happiness, empathy, and support; a private place of escape in which to rest, relax, and renew; something to hold on to when all else seems to be slipping away. Wrapping another in a shawl knit of your own prayers and loving thoughts is a gift not only for the one receiving the shawl but for yourself as well. Here we'll show you how to turn your shawl making into an experience that blesses everyone involved.

Prayer begins in the heart. Because the creation of a prayer shawl is, first, a spiritual practice for the shawl maker, it's important to set an environment of intention, or purpose, as you begin.

Thinking about Who Will Wear the Shawl

The first step in establishing intention occurs when you hear of a need or are inspired to reach out to another person in his or her time of difficulty or celebration—a family member, friend, neighbor, acquaintance, or even someone you've never met but heard about from others. We encourage you to "trust the shawl." It will go to just the right person and arrive at just the right time. Often enough, it happens that when we start out knitting a shawl with a particular person in mind, a more urgent need arises and someone else needs it even more. Or there are times when we begin a shawl with no recipient in mind, believing that the person who needs it will eventually come into our lives. Once you get started, we have no doubt that you will find this to be true for you, too.

Choosing Yarn

When we begin knitting any project for another person, we plan it with that person in mind. What are the recipient's favorite colors? What fiber will feel best against his or her skin? When we choose yarn for a prayer shawl, the process is no different. Whether you know the recipient of your shawl or not, consider first the color or colors you will use, as they will have an effect on the recipient. Bright colors such as red or gold generally uplift and energize, as seen in

the Mexican Rainbow Shawl (p. 48) and Alice's Lace Shawl (p. 148); dark colors often give a sense of escape and enfolding, as they do in Carri Hammett's Lap Robe (p. 120). And as illustrated by Jodi Lewanda's Calming Shawl (p. 42), neutrals and pastels tend to be comforting. See "Color & Symbology," on p. 164 to learn about the symbolic meanings associated with colors or let your intuition be your guide. Once you've chosen the colors, trust your selection—it will be right for the person who receives it.

Next, consider the type of yarn you will use. If you're making a shawl with an intricate pattern or are knitting for someone with simple taste, you might prefer a smooth, worsted-weight yarn to emphasize the design. When the pattern is plain and texture is the focus, you may wish to use a knobby bouclé or other type of novelty yarn. Higher-end yarns, such as hand-painted yarns and those made with luxury fibers, may be desired for very special shawls, perhaps one intended for a dear friend. Some shawl makers use remnants of yarn— mixing colors, types, and textures—to create dramatic, one-of-a-kind shawls known as Joseph's coat shawls, oddball shawls, gypsy shawls, patchwork shawls, or *anawim* shawls (a Hebrew word meaning "God's faithful remnant"). Brandon Mably's Striped Stole (p. 124) and the Traveling Shawl (p. 132) are beautiful examples. Once you're comfortable with the shawl-making process, we encourage you to experiment with color, pattern, and yarn. Allow yourself to be inspired, express your creativity, and enjoy the experience.

Creating the Environment

You may not realize it, but everything we've talked about up to now is part of the spiritual experience of making a shawl. Of course, the actual knitting is much more intensely spiritual, so it's important to take the time to set the mood. In doing so, consider creating a small ritual that is meaningful to you. Here are a few suggestions that have worked nicely for us.

Before you sit down to begin, gather together:

- Yarn
- Tools
- Candle and matches
- Journal and pen
- Favorite prayer, poem, or reading

You may also wish to have the following:

- Mild scented hand lotion (unless your shawl recipient is sensitive to smells or allergic to such products)
- Something to drink (perhaps a cup of tea)
- Music (a favorite CD or a radio station that plays soothing or meditative music)

Find a quiet spot and get comfortable. The ideal is away from the TV in a peaceful place either inside or outside. Then, begin as follows:

- Sit quietly for a moment.
- Take a few deep breaths to relax.
- Center yourself and reflect on what you're about to do.
- Light the candle and massage the lotion into your hands to prepare them for the task ahead.
- Record the date in your journal and, as you knit, jot down insights, thoughts, and reflections that come to you. You may wish to include these in a note you give to the person who receives your shawl; they might also be the beginnings of a prayer, blessing, or poem. Some groups that co-knit a shawl keep a journal of their collective experience and include the journal with the shawl when it's given away.
- Place your hand on the yarn, recite a blessing, read a poem or prayer, or just sit quietly for a moment.
- If you've chosen music, play it softly in the background.
- Begin casting on your stitches.

As you work, think about or pray for the person who will receive your shawl. Remember being swaddled in a blanket as a child. Recall the feeling of utter bliss and complete surrender when being enfolded by someone who cares for you. Pray those memories into your knitting along with thoughts of strength, peace, and healing for the one who will receive the work of your hands. Make this process an extension of your life and the desires of your heart. Rest assured that the energy you impart will be felt.

Usually, you will take your time making a shawl, finding bits of time in your day when you can calmly and prayerfully work on it. Sometimes you'll work in solitude, but you may often find yourself weaving the pattern of your life into the pattern of the shawl as it accompanies you to meetings, appointments, soccer games, and gatherings.

You'll find that folks are interested in what you're doing. As you explain, little seeds of interest are planted (and so the ministry grows). Of course, there may be occasions when you are under time constraints and need to speed up the shawl-making process. We have found that emergency situations— such as accidents, urgent surgeries, or a sudden death—can sometimes cut short the time we thought we had to work on a shawl, so we'll enlist a few friends or our group to help, passing the work from one person to another.

Adding Embellishment

After you've finished the body of the shawl, you may decide to embellish it with fringe or tassels. This too can be an occasion for prayer. Some people tie a knot into various pieces of fringe as they work, keeping the intentions of the receiver in mind or saying a prayer for her or him as they do. Members of some Prayer Shawl Ministry groups take turns tying a knot in each others' shawls to add their prayers, as well.

Charms and beads also add to a shawl's beauty and can be a source of meditation. Hearts, angels, and religious symbols are popular choices, but consider others. If you know the recipient of the shawl, you can add some significant symbols or colorful beads that connect the two of you. For example, add a flower charm if you both enjoy gardening or a seashell if you share a love of the ocean.

If the shawl is a gift from a group, invite everyone to add his or her own tokens of affection and remembrances. Encourage recipients to add beads or charms of their own, perhaps something that belonged to family members or friends. A locket with a picture of a loved one is a personal touch as well. If the recipient is Catholic, then adding 10 beads to each side of the shawl would enable the wearer to say a few decades of the rosary. For more ideas, see "Color & Symbology" on p. 164.

Blessing the Shawl

When the shawl is completed, offer up a final blessing before it is sent on its way. If you belong to a group, gather around the finished shawl, lay your hands on it, and say a blessing in unison. Some groups bless their shawls once a month in church. This is a great way to include the members of the congregation who don't knit or crochet. You or your group may wish to write your own blessing, or you may choose a favorite poem, prayer, or benediction. You can get lots of ideas from our website (www.shawlministry.com).

Then, before you give the shawl away, think about what words you'd like to include with it. Revisit your journal and, if you wish, attach a note, tag, or card that answers the following questions:

- What is a prayer shawl?
- Why has the shawl been given away?
- Who is giving the shawl?

Each person or group may decide what to say to a shawl's recipient. Some groups write detailed letters to explain the meanings of the color and other symbolism (such as the number of stitches in the pattern or the significance of the charms added) along with a blessing. Sometimes a tag with a blessing is tied to the fringe; occasionally, groups special-order cloth labels that identify the group or organization and are sewn onto a corner of the shawl. Or you may simply include a handwritten, from-the-heart card.

Presenting a Shawl

Depending on the circumstances, there are many ways of presenting a shawl. If you are delivering a shawl by yourself and in person, you may simply give the shawl to the one it's intended for, explaining what it is and why you want her or him to have it. If you feel comfortable, consider saying a little blessing, prayer, or poem as you drape the shawl around the person's shoulders. Don't worry if the person doesn't seem as receptive as you'd

like—sometimes it takes a while for it all to sink in. This might become an opportunity for quiet conversation, reflection, or even shared tears. What's most important is that it is a sacred moment in which the giver, the receiver, and others present are blessed.

This is not as easy as it sounds for many of us. We may feel uncomfortable or awkward around others who are in pain or experiencing grief. What are we supposed to say? What if we say the wrong thing? What if we unintentionally cause the person more pain? It's normal to worry about these things. But you don't have to know all the right words to make this a meaningful moment. Your very presence, your willingness to listen, and your shawl will be enough. If the person receiving the shawl begins to cry, or even wishes to talk, simple responses such as nodding, touching a hand or shoulder, asking a specific question or two, or making a small comment to show you are listening are entirely appropriate. Listening and simply being present with the person are the best gifts you can offer.

If a group of friends are presenting the shawl, it's lovely to have the recipient stand (if possible) or sit in the middle of the group, then have everyone place a hand on the shawl as you read the blessing in unison. Our first shawl, for a friend going through a divorce, was presented in this manner. We gathered together a group of sister friends, each of us taking turns wrapping up in the shawl and sharing a blessing, either spoken aloud or silently in our hearts. As it was wrapped around our friend's shoulders, she was told of the prayers and good wishes that had been prayed into it by those who cared for her.

Always let the circumstances, the place, and the personality of the person who is to receive your shawl be your guide. What we've described is a wonderful opportunity of sharing and blessing for all involved. Make sure there is enough time for this ritual.

On the other hand, there will be occasions when you won't be involved in a formal presentation. Sometimes shawls are picked up by family members or friends, or they're sent by mail. However the shawl is received, trust that it will be a sacred moment, and one that happens at just the right time.

Finally, regardless of how the wrap is presented, there are a few things to keep in mind when packaging a shawl for presentation and delivery. Here are some ideas for packaging your shawls in an attractive—but practical—manner:

• Place it in a 2-gallon sealable plastic bag. These are especially handy for less personal deliveries to hospitals, nursing homes, and so on. They are easy to store and hold everything you wish to include with the shawl, such as tags, letters, cards, and sachets.

• Place it in a decorative gift bag when you're giving someone his or her shawl in person. Gift bags, though less durable, can also hold other items you'd like to include.

• Hand sew, knit, or crochet a pouch from remnants of fabric or yarn. This type of bag creates a little pillow when the shawl is stored in it.

• Simply wrap the shawl in pretty tissue paper, wrapping paper, or fabric, tied with a piece of yarn.

Receiving a Shawl

All prayer shawl makers are eager to be givers, but we encourage you to allow yourself to be a willing recipient as well, if the occasion arises. There's a certain amount of letting go in allowing someone else to minister to you, and this can be a welcome relief to a shawl maker who is always on the giving end. We hope the time comes when someone gives you a shawl so that you may welcome the full-circle blessings of being both giver and receiver.

Gentle Shawl Making

Gentle shawl making is how we describe less physically demanding knitting practices for those of us with health issues that impede our knitting—carpal tunnel syndrome, fibromyalgia, arthritis, and others. If knitting is physically difficult for you, but you'd still like to participate in the Prayer Shawl Ministry, start simply, slowly, and prayerfully. Do what you can in small blocks of time, putting the work aside when you need a rest. You may want to do just part of a shawl and pass it on to someone else. Or you could prayerfully concentrate on the fringe or border of a shawl that someone else has made. The most important component of this ministry is prayer, which doesn't require any physical strength, just a desire of the heart.

If you would like to make prayer shawls, but are hesitant to do so because of health concerns, please reconsider. We have received inspiring e-mails from shawl makers with health challenges who say that being involved in this ministry helps them focus on others, remain active, and stay connected to their faith community. Their shawl-making process may have its limits, but the benefits are limitless.

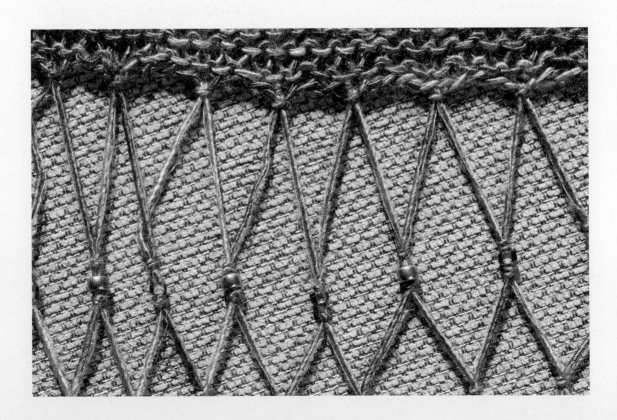

T**HIS SHAWL IS A METAPHOR FOR FRIENDSHIP.**

FROM
Janet Bristow

In keeping with the symbolism of threes, it is made with three stitches. Garter Stitch is a dependable, basic stitch. Stockinette Stitch is a mainstay, combining the smooth knitted stitch on one side and the bumpier purl on the other. Seed Stitch takes time and focus. We all have friends who fit these categories. Each one is unique and treasured. This shawl is very adaptable in that the shawl maker can use any color and type of yarn, or three stitch types. The multiple strands are knit together, symbolizing the friendship two people share, but the shawl can be made with a single strand as long as the needle size is adjusted to fit the yarn.

FRIENDSHIP PATCHWORK SHAWL

Skill Level
Easy

Finished Measurements
60 in long and 20 in wide

Yarn
Note: This amount of yarn will make two shawls—enough to share with a friend. If you wish to make only one shawl, simply divide the required yarn amounts in half.
- 500 yd worsted weight yarn (Color A)
- 500 yd worsted weight yarn (Color B)
- 750 yd bulky bouclé yarn
- 60 yd bulky novelty yarn
- Shawl shown in Caron® Simply Soft (100% acrylic; 330 yd/6 oz), 2 skeins #9738 Violet; Red Heart® Soft Yarn™ (100% acrylic; 256 yd/5 oz), 2 skeins #9537 Fuchsia; Bernat® Soft Bouclé (97% acrylic/3% polyester; 255 yd/5 oz), 3 skeins #26960 Crazy Shades; Patons® Carmen (36% polyester/64% nylon; 64 yd/1.75 oz), 1 skein #07310 Violet

Needles
- Size 17 or 19 straight or circular needles (or size needed to obtain gauge)

Gauge
- 10 sts and 10 rows = 4 in worked in Stockinette Stitch
- 14 sts and 12 rows = 4 in worked in Garter Stitch
- 10 sts and 14 rows = 4 in worked in Seed Stitch

FRIENDSHIP PATCHWORK SHAWL

DIRECTIONS

Note: Row numbers are approx. Feel free to adjust number of rows you knit with the different yarn combinations.

With 2 strands Color A and 1 strand novelty yarn held tog, CO on 43 sts or number for desired width (being sure number of sts is odd).

Row 1: Knit across.

Rows 2–9: Drop novelty yarn. With 2 strands Color A, knit all rows (Garter Stitch).

Row 10: Drop Color A. With 2 strands Color B, k1, p1 across (Seed Stitch).

Rows 11–16: Knit the purl sts and purl the knit sts as they face you.

Rows 17–29: Drop Color B. With 2 strands bouclé, knit all odd rows and purl all even rows (Stockinette Stitch).

Continue working Rows 1–29, adding novelty yarn for 2 rows whenever you choose, until shawl measures approx 60 in. **Note:** Length of shawl can be wrist-to-wrist or fingertip-to-fingertip, if desired.

BO all sts and add fringe (see pp. 167–168) using 16-in strands of each yarn for each fringe as follows: 1 strand novelty, 2 strands bouclé, and 2 strands each of Colors A and B.

KNITTED IN LOVE

Friendship, like a shawl
Is colorful and warm
Enfolding the good times
Sheltering difficulties.

Knitted in love,
Like the Garter Stitch
The one you learn first, always there for you
Easy, basic, dependable.
Creator God, keep me from taking friends
for granted.

Knitted in peace
It's a place of solace and challenge
Like the Stockinette Stitch
Smooth on the front, bumpy on the back
Mantle of Love, help me to appreciate the one,
Be patient with the other.

Knitted in hope
This special gift is
Like the Seed Stitch,
Requiring attention and commitment,
focus and skill.
Comforter, plant in me the wisdom
to cherish it.

Friendship, like a shawl
Is worn in gratitude and with pride
As we are embraced in its weavings.
Divine shelter, we glimpse you!

—JANET BRISTOW

Soul Sisters

Jeanette came into my life as a special gift from the Creator. She was my soul mate and a spiritual companion. She battled with cancer, and as she did, she taught me how to live daily in grace-filled moments. Jeanette saw God working in every dimension of her life, whether she was listening to her favorite music, working in her flower garden, or preparing meals for her family. The ability to listen to others was the fuel that brought her calm and enlightenment.

When we visited, we prayed and wrapped ourselves in our prayer shawls, their fringes tangling together as we held hands. We spoke about our spiritual experiences, and we admired the special beads and symbols attached to the fringes of our shawls, including some she had received from her daughters, Laura and Alice, and her grandchildren. The fringe also included a handmade signet ring from her father-in-law. All these items gave Jeanette the feeling of a deep spiritual connectedness with her loved ones. Each of our shawls also had a decade of the rosary that I had added to the fringes, so we could finger the beads as we prayed Hail Marys. This ritual filled us with tranquility and courage, even as we shared our inner thoughts and cried,

knowing her beautiful journey of life would come to an end much too quickly. Our prayer shawls had created a unique and lasting bond between two like-minded women.

One day, Jeanette asked me if the prayer shawl I had knitted so prayerfully and lovingly for her could be used as her burial shroud. Without hesitation, I agreed. When the end of her life arrived, her husband, Anthony, gave instructions that Jeanette's prayer shawl be laid out to cover her from head to foot. With this act, we felt that the shawl had been transformed into the arms of the Lord, embracing Jeanette and guiding her to meet all the loved ones who had passed before her.

Death does not separate soul sisters. Those we knit shawls for are never at a distance because we remember that this unassuming act of love—knitting for another—can have great power in our lives. The secret is to teach ourselves to stay present to the moment, to knit *for* the person, known or unknown. The knitting of a prayer shawl is truly a gift, a positive action that can be shared with those we encounter in our daily world. I have abundant daily reminders of Jeanette, and in them, ever so slightly, the fringes of our shawls seem to touch each other once again.

GLADYS COLE, Nokomis, Florida

FROM
Dee Jones
Nevada City, California

L IVING IN NEVADA CITY IN THE HEART OF THE SIERRA foothills is like living in another century," writes Donna Foote, participant in the Nevada City United Methodist Church Shawl Ministry and blessing writer for this light-and-lacy mohair shawl. "The town looks almost like it did during the California Gold Rush. The first Methodist church in Nevada City burned to the ground when the entire town went up in flames on a wild Saturday night. Undaunted by adversity, the faithful rebuilt. Every time I walk into the sanctuary, I hear those voices of the past and picture miners, merchants, and townspeople huddled together singing God's praises before picking up their hammers to build anew. I especially envision those hearty pioneer women, wrapped tightly in their shawls on a frosty morning, listening to the preacher talk of a new day. If only those shawls could speak." Certainly your prayer shawls have stories, too. As you knit, consider what they might say if they could.

SIERRA BREEZE

Skill Level
Intermediate

Finished Measurements
70 in long and 28 in wide

Yarn
- Approx 675 yd mohair yarn
- Shawl shown in Mountain Colors Mohair (78% mohair/13% wool/9% nylon; 225 yd/3.5 oz), 3 skeins North Winds

Needles
- Size 13 straight or circular needles for body (or size needed to obtain gauge)
- Size 15 straight or circular needles for CO and BO

Notions
- Stitch markers
- Stainless-steel pins

Gauge
- 12 sts and 14 rows = 4 in worked in Stockinette Stitch

THE PIONEER SHAWL

I am a shawl and I have a story to tell.
I once covered the shoulders of a young bride
heading west.
I felt the prairie wind
whipping
stinging
buffeting.

I warmed her body underneath starry skies
And worked extra hard at dawn
keeping her warm
While she toiled and waited for the sun to rise.

I was a basket for fresh-picked flowers
And a pillow when she lay in the prairie grass
looking at the sky
Dreaming of the day when she could
wear her shawl
With a new dress.

I clung to her shaking body as she
tossed soft dirt
On a new-made grave
And heard her silent prayer for his
salvation and peace.

I'm a true pioneer. I'm tough. I've seen it all.
And I still keep
comforting
binding
uniting
Us all in a blessed feeling of kinship
and shared connection.

—DONNA FOOTE
GRASS VALLEY, CALIFORNIA

SIERRA BREEZE

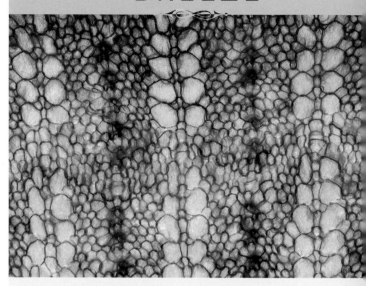

RIPPLE LACE PATTERN

Note: Work Double Decrease as follows: Sl 2 sts tog knitwise, k1, pass 2 slipped sts over.

Row 1 (RS): P2, k2tog, *k3, yo, k1, yo, k3, work Double Decrease. Repeat from * twice. K3, yo, k1, yo, k3, k2tog, p2. **Note:** The last k2tog in this row is *not* a Double Decrease.

Row 2: K2, purl to last 2 sts of lace panel, k2.

Rows 3–10: Repeat Rows 1 and 2 for 4 times more. (You will have 5 holes in the lacy column.)

Row 11: P2, k1, *p4, k1. Repeat from * to last 2 sts of lace panel, end p2.

Row 12: Repeat Row 2.

Row 13: P2, knit to last 2 sts of lace panel, p2.

Row 14: K7, p1 (k4, p1) 6 times, k7.

DIRECTIONS
Using larger needles, CO 85 sts.
Change to smaller needles. Knit 5 rows.

BODY
Row 1 (RS): K20, place marker, work Row 1 of Ripple Lace Pattern, place marker, k20.

Row 2: K5, purl to marker, work Row 2 of Ripple Lace Pattern, purl to last 5 sts, end k5.

Repeat these 2 rows, progressing through all 14 rows of Ripple Lace Pattern at the same time.

Repeat these 2 rows and Ripple Lace Pattern until shawl is nearly desired length. After Row 9 of last repeat of Ripple Lace Pattern, remove markers and begin border as follows: Beginning on WS, knit 4 rows. Change to larger needles, knit 1 row. BO *loosely*.

FINISHING
If desired, block to accentuate the lace scallops (there will be 3 at beginning of shawl, 4 at end). To block, lay shawl over large towels on a flat surface (a carpet or bed) where it will be undisturbed. Pin all around shawl with stainless-steel (rustproof) pins, stretching slightly to allow the lace pattern to open up. Pin scallops down well, shaping them evenly as you do. Spritz well with a hand mister and allow to dry thoroughly (this may take more than a day, depending on climate).

The Blanket

Every year on the first day of school, I used to read my kindergartners a book about Susi, whose best friend is her blue blanket. It's a cape, a secret fort—whatever her imagination desires. Mostly, it protects and comforts her when she is scared or unsure. She can't imagine being without her cuddly companion. She knows kindergarten is going to be so cool, but she isn't sure she is ready to make that change and leave her blanket behind. In the end, she comes up with a plan. She cuts a small corner off her blue blanket to carry in her backpack; no one but Susi will know that it's there.

Like Susi, many times we try to hold on to familiar things when a change comes. We forget, though, that change can be a good thing. This past year, I stopped teaching to become the youth director at my church. The day I put all of my teaching things into storage, I felt a sense of unrest. Was this change really the right thing? I felt like Susi facing kindergarten without her blanket.

That night, I went to my parents' house for dinner. My mom presented me with a prayer shawl that a woman at church had made for me. She pulled it out of the bag and put it on me. I couldn't believe it. The shawl was the same color as Susi's blanket from the story. I felt that God was reminding me that the things I was giving up could still be with me, just in a new way. Like Susi, I discovered a new way to carry what was important with me on my faith journey.

KIRSTEN ERICKSON, Seattle, Washington

AD LIB SHAWL

A BELOVED SHAWL AND A LITTLE "AD LIB" LED TO Kristin Spurkland's sweet and folksy triangular wrap. The body of the shawl is a simple knit—and it's fun to watch the colors change as the piece grows. The short-row shaping allows for a snug fit around the shoulders and provides a bit of a challenge for a knitter ready to try something more than straightforward knitting and purling. Instructions are given for both a solid-color shawl and the multicolored version you see here.

Skill Level
Intermediate

Finished Measurements
61 in long and 26 in deep

Yarn
- Approx 700 yd DK weight yarn (for single-color shawl)
- Approx 450 yd DK weight yarn, plus small amounts of 5 other colors (for multicolored shawl)
- Shawl shown in Hifa Ullgarn (100% wool; 228 yd/3.5 oz), 2 skeins #6097 Ballet Pink (Color A), small amounts of each of the following: #6073 Rose (Color B), #6018 Berry (Color C), #6029 Teal (Color D), #6090 Olive (Color E), and #6089 Spinach (Color F)

Needles
- Size 7 circular needle, 24 in to 29 in long (or size needed to obtain gauge)

Notions
- Stitch marker
- Tapestry needle

Gauge
- 18 sts and 34 rows = 4 in worked in Garter Stitch
- Exact gauge is not crucial. Gauge at start of shawl tends to be tighter than final gauge at top because fabric stretches as shawl gets larger and heavier.

KRISTIN SPURKLAND'S
AD LIB SHAWL

DIRECTIONS

Note: These directions are for a simple, single-color triangular shawl with short-row shaping at the top edge. The short rows help the shawl stay on the shoulders.

With Color A, CO 5 sts.

Setup Row: Kf&b, knit to last 2 sts, kf&b, k1. (7 sts)

Place marker in center st. (You'll need to know where it is when you start short rows at top, and it's easier to mark it now. Also, having center st marked helps keep incs on track because you can periodically check that you have same number of sts on either side of center st.)

Note: If you are making multicolored version, begin Color Sequence here.

Row 1 (RS): Knit.

Row 2 (WS): Kf&b, knit to last 2 sts, kf&b, k1.

Repeat Rows 1 and 2 until you have 223 sts.

SHOULDER SHAPING

Note: The short rows in this shawl are worked differently from the usual technique. If you are a short-row expert, feel free to use your favorite method. For those familiar with short-row techniques, note that the wraps in this technique are not picked up and worked with the slipped sts when reactivating sts.

When working short rows, continue to inc at edges as established.

Setup Row: Knit to 9 sts from marked center st. Turn work, move yarn to back of work, sl first st on left needle purlwise, knit to last 2 sts, kf&b, k1.

Note: The place where you turned and slipped the st is a called the *turning point*.

Short-Row Sequence:
*Knit to 10 sts from last turning point, turn work, move yarn to back of work, sl first st on left needle purlwise, knit to last 2 sts, kf&b, k1.

Repeat from * until you have worked 11 turning points total, ending with a WS row completed.

Next Row (RS): Knit all sts.

Set up for short rows on second side: Kf&b, knit to 9 sts from marked center st. Turn work, move yarn to back of work, sl first st on left needle purlwise, knit to end of row.

Short-Row Sequence:
*Kf&b, knit to 10 sts from last turning point, turn work, move yarn to back of work, sl first st on left needle purlwise, knit to end of row.

Repeat from * until you have worked 11 turning points total, ending with a RS row completed.

Next Row (WS):
Kf&b, knit to last 2 sts, kf&b, k1.

BO in k1, p1. (This creates a subtle texture along BO edge, which works nicely with Garter Stitch and short-row turns, while adding elasticity to edge.)

continued

KRISTIN SPURKLAND'S
AD LIB SHAWL

OPTIONAL COLOR SEQUENCE

Note: Each ridge is made up of Rows 1 and 2. So if directions say to work 4 ridges in Color A, you will knit a total of 8 rows in that color. Color changes should always occur on Row 1, the RS row.

CO and work Setup Row in Color A, then work Color Sequence as follows:

7 ridges Color A	2 ridges Color C
2 ridges Color B	1 ridge Color E
1 ridge Color C	6 ridges Color A
5 ridges Color A	1 ridge Color E
1 ridge Color D	1 ridge Color D
1 ridge Color A	12 ridges Color A
1 ridge Color E	1 ridge Color B
2 ridges Color F	4 ridges Color A
10 ridges Color A	2 ridges Color B
1 ridge Color B	1 ridge Color E
1 ridge Color D	1 ridge Color C
2 ridges Color B	1 ridge Color D
1 ridge Color C	1 ridge Color F
1 ridge Color A	1 ridge Color D
2 ridges Color E	2 ridges Color A
4 ridges Color A	1 ridge Color D
1 ridge Color D	6 ridges Color A
7 ridges Color A	2 ridges Color C
2 ridges Color F	1 ridge Color B
1 ridge Color A	1 ridge Color A
1 ridge Color B	1 ridge Color F
1 ridge Color A	4 ridges Color A

After completing Color Sequence, begin short-row shaping as in basic directions, working remainder of shawl in Color A.

MEDITATION

We are what we think.
All that we are arises with our thoughts.
With our thoughts, we make our world.

—BUDDHA

Tante's Stash Shawl

I based my design on a shawl knit for me by one of my Norwegian *tante* (aunts) when I was a girl. A stash project for sure, it's a simple navy blue Garter Stitch triangle broken up by random stripes in red, yellow, white, heathered blue and gray, light blue, and orange.

As an admirer of the elegant simplicity of that shawl, I've long wanted to re-create it in my own palette. When the call came out for contributions to this book, I took it as the cue to finally knit my version of my tante's stash shawl.

Despite my appreciation of the free-form nature of the original, I immediately sat down and starting planning the color sequence for my version. Working at my computer, I created a variety of stripe sequences, some based on mathematical concepts, some approached more intuitively, but all very structured. I then swatched the various sequences that appealed to me the most.

None of them worked.

In fact, the beauty of the original lies in its spontaneity. To successfully re-create my own version, I had to be willing to improvise. So improvise I did, knitting for a while with the base color (a soft pink, in my version), then thinking, "How about working a couple rows of rose now?" I did not allow myself the option of stopping to analyze my work and make adjustments. Once I chose a color, there was no ripping out, no second-guessing. That was it: I was committed.

This worked.

A rather obvious metaphor is embedded in this experience. Although some degree of planning and goal setting is of course necessary and wise, too much future gazing can limit our capacity to respond to life's unscheduled events with spontaneity, wonder, perhaps even enjoyment. Being able to accept what comes and continue onward is a valuable skill, worth practicing often.

To knit this shawl as intended—without a set plan, letting the colors flow as they will—is to engage the skill of being in the moment, and it encourages a loosening of our grip on how things "should be." The flexibility to take what comes with openness and acceptance is what I considered as I worked this design, which I have titled Ad Lib.

KRISTIN SPURKLAND, Portland, Oregon

FROM
Catherine Izard
Trondheim, Norway & Susan Izard
West Hartford, Connecticut

SUSAN IZARD, ASSOCIATE PASTOR OF SPIRITUAL
life at First Church of Christ Congregational, West Hartford,
Connecticut, and co-author of *Knitting into the Mystery*, designed this shawl with
her daughter, Catherine. The pattern is based on seven stitches, hence the name
Sabbath Shawl.

SABBATH SHAWL

Skill Level
Experienced

Finished Measurements
57½ in long and 17½ in wide

Yarn
• Approx 750 yd smooth DK weight yarn in
  a natural fiber (wool, silk, cotton, or linen)
• Shawl shown in Sublime Cashmere
  Merino Silk DK (75% extra-fine
  merino/20% silk/5% cashmere;
  127 yd/1.75 oz), 6 skeins #11 Clove
Note: Synthetic fibers (such as acrylic)
will not block well; textured yarns may
obscure stitch pattern.

Needles
• Size 8 straight or circular needles
  (or size needed to obtain gauge)

Notions
• Stitch markers
• Dental floss and thin cotton yarn
• Stainless-steel pins

Gauge
• 16 sts and 24 rows = 4 in worked in Lace
  Pattern, blocked
• Experiment with your yarn by knitting a
  small swatch on different needle sizes
  until you get a tension you like.

Notes
• Blocking is essential for knitted lace;
  instructions are provided.
• For a wider shawl, increase st count by
  increments of 7 and add repeats of
  Lace Pattern.
• Beginning lace knitters should place a
  marker between every repeat of the Lace
  Pattern. On purl rows, make sure there
  are 7 sts between each marker. Also, insert
  a "lifeline" every 10 or 12 rows. After you
  finish a row, thread a needle with dental
  floss and run it through sts on needle.
  This way, if you make a mistake you will
  have to unravel knitting only back to
  lifeline rather than to beginning.

SABBATH SHAWL

DIRECTIONS

CO 85 sts.

Rows 1–6: Work in Seed Stitch as follows: *K1, p1, repeat from * to end of row. (After Row 1, for Seed Stitch, knit the purl sts and purl the knit sts as they face you.)

Row 7: Purl.

Row 8 (Begin Lace Pattern): Work 4 sts in Seed Stitch, place marker, (k1, k2tog, yo, k, yo, ssk, k) 11 times, place marker, work 4 sts in Seed Stitch.

Row 9: Work 4 sts in Seed Stitch, p77, work 4 sts in Seed Stitch.

Row 10: Work 4 sts in Seed Stitch, (k2tog, yo, k3, yo, ssk) 11 times, work 4 sts in Seed Stitch.

Row 11: Work 4 sts in Seed Stitch, p77, work 4 sts in Seed Stitch.

Repeat Rows 8–11 until shawl is as long as desired. End with a WS (purl) row.

Work 6 rows in Seed Stitch.

BO very loosely, using a larger needle if necessary.

FINISHING

1. Weave in ends, but do not cut yarn.

2. Thread a needle with a piece of thin cotton yarn (or butcher's twine) about twice as long as shawl. Run yarn through very edge of long side of shawl through each of bumps made by purl sts.

3. Fill a bucket or sink with lukewarm water with a little bit of baby shampoo. (*Do not* use Woolite or other special detergents because they may damage the fibers.)

4. Soak shawl for at least 20 minutes, until it is saturated and fibers have relaxed.

5. While shawl is soaking, cover a bed (or other surface you can pin fabric to) with a clean white sheet. (The shawl should take less than a day to dry.)

6. Being very careful not to let bits of shawl dangle or stretch, transfer shawl to a colander and *gently* press out as much water as you can. Do not twist or wring.

7. If shawl is still dirty or if there is bleeding, repeat washing process until water runs clear.

8. Lay out a thick towel. Again, without stretching knitting, spread out shawl on towel. Lay another towel on top and roll all layers together. Stand, sit, or lean on roll to wring out water. You want shawl to be damp, but not dry.

9. Bring roll over to bed and *carefully* lay shawl out.

10. Pin out both ends of one cotton string so that string is very taut. This may take many pins.

11. Pin down one corner of shawl along cotton string.

12. Pulling gently to open up Lace Pattern, pin down the corner that is diagonal to the one already pinned. You can be firm with the yarn, but be gentle. (Be more careful with alpaca yarn because it is not as elastic as wool.)

13. Now that you have established width of shawl, repeat pinning with other cotton string.

14. Pin remaining two corners, forming a rectangle.

15. Placing pins about 1 in apart, fasten short sides of shawl so it is straight.

16. Let shawl dry completely (or all your hard work blocking will be for naught).

17. After shawl is dry, unpin and cut ends. Carefully remove cotton string.

BLESSING OF THE SABBATH SHAWL

When wrapped in your Sabbath shawl
may the God of rest embrace you;
may the Christ of gentleness encircle you;
may the Spirit of truth guide you.

When wrapped in your Sabbath shawl
may the God of stillness encompass you;
may the Christ of reflection inspire you;
may the Spirit of wisdom provide for you.

When wrapped in your Sabbath shawl
may the God of silence surround you;
may the Christ of renewal encourage you;
may the Spirit of life companion you.

When wrapped in your Sabbath shawl
may the God of love dwell with you this
day and evermore. Amen.

—SUSAN IZARD
WEST HARTFORD, CONNECTICUT

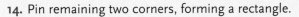

Love Matters

Carolyn, a member of our knitting ministry, is friends with a woman named Margaret who lives in Carolyn's assisted-living community. Margaret, who is Jewish, is a concentration camp survivor, and of her whole family, only she and her brother made it through the camps and the second World War.

Recently, Margaret was faced with another challenge to survive: cancer. When Carolyn found out, she wanted to reach out to her friend. She had a shawl she had knit some years before and decided to give it to Margaret. The next day, she took the shawl to her friend, who was so touched by this gift that she wore the shawl everywhere. She even wore it one Sunday when she came to a service at our church with Carolyn. Afterward, she sent me a card, thanking me personally for this ministry that supplies so many people with prayer shawls like hers.

Over her lifetime, Margaret has known what it means to be castigated for her faith. It must be a remarkable thing to be wrapped in a prayer shawl made by a dear friend and know that her religious tradition doesn't matter—what matters is love.

SUSAN IZARD, West Hartford, Connecticut

FROM
Linn Walck
Venice, Florida

WHEN ASKED TO CONTRIBUTE A NEW DESIGN to the Prayer Shawl Ministry," writes designer Linn Walck, a member of the Prayer Shawl Ministry group of Epiphany Cathedral in Venice, Florida, "I thought about a shawl pattern that would incorporate and represent the Seven Sacraments in the Catholic tradition. At a baby's Baptism, such a shawl would be draped around the parents and child to bond them as one in faith. It would be carried again at First Communion and Confirmation. As with the custom in many South American countries of binding a newly married couple with a cord, the shawl would be used [at a wedding] to signify a couple's new unity. On Ordination Day, the shawl would be carried by the mother of the new priest or deacon. At the Sacrament of the Sick, it would be draped on the shoulders or placed on the lap of the person who was ill. The Seed Stitch portrays the seeds that blossom into a faith that continues to grow throughout the years. The blocks of three in the motif represent the Trinity. The seven motifs across the shawl are for the Seven Sacraments."

SEVEN SACRAMENTS

Skill Level
Intermediate

Finished Measurements
24 in by 69 in, excluding fringe

Yarn
- Approx 1,400 yd sport weight yarn
- Shawl shown in Bernat Softee Baby (100% acrylic; 455 yd/5 oz), 4 skeins #02000 White

Needles
- Size 8 straight or circular needles (or size needed to obtain gauge)
- Size D crochet hook for attaching fringe

Notions
- Stitch markers

Gauge
- 20 sts and 24 rows = 4 in worked in Cross Pattern

SEVEN SACRAMENTS

EYELET HEM
CO 124 sts.

Beginning with a purl row, work
3 rows in Stockinette Stitch
(knit 1 row, purl 1 row).

Next row (RS):
*K1, yo, k2tog; repeat from * across.

Beginning with a purl row, work
3 rows in Stockinette Stitch.
Note: After the hem is folded at the
eyelet row and sewn down,
a scalloped edge will be seen;
the eyelets will hold the fringe.

SEED STITCH BORDER
Rows 1, 3, 5, and 7: K1, p1.

Rows 2, 4, 6, and 8: P1, k1.

Rows 9–12: K4, *yo, k2tog; repeat
from *, end k4.

Rows 13, 15, 17, and 19: K1, p1.

Rows 14, 16, 18, and 20: P1, k1.

BODY (Cross Pattern)
Place a marker after the
first 4 sts and before
the last 4 sts; maintain
Seed Stitch Border over
these 4 sts on either end.
Between markers, work
Cross Pattern as follows:

Rows 1–4: K4, *yo,
k2tog; repeat from *,
end k4.

Rows 5–8: K4, (yo,
k2tog) twice, *k4, p4,
k4; (yo, k2tog) twice,
repeat from *, end k4.

Rows 9–12: K4, (yo,
k2tog) twice; *p4, k4,
p4; (yo,k2tog) twice,
repeat from *, end k4.

Rows 13–16: K4, (yo,
k2tog) twice; *k4, p4,
k4; (yo,k2tog) twice,
repeat from *, end k4.

Rows 17–20: K4,*yo,
k2tog; repeat from *,
end k4.

Rows 21–24: K4, work
Seed Stitch, end k4.

Repeat until piece
measures 68 in, or
desired length, from
eyelet row. End with
Row 18 of Cross Pattern.
Repeat Seed Stitch
Border, then repeat
Eyelet Hem, reversing
knit and purl rows so all
sewing is on the same

side. Beginning with a knit row, work 3 rows in Stockinette Stitch, 1 eyelet row, and 3 rows in Stockinette Stitch. BO knitwise.

FINISHING

Fold each end at eyelet row and sew to WS. Using crochet hook, attach three 9-in strands of yarn, making fringe, in each k2tog hole on the fold (see p. 167).

(see p. 167)

WE KNIT

We take up our needles and yarn . . .
And . . . we knit.
God took earth, sea, and sky
To create this world.
He knitted it all together, and . . .
Said, "It is good."

We knit . . . stitch by stitch . . .
To create a garment of love.
God's love surrounds us as
We knit . . . and pray.

Row by row, and prayer by prayer,
In a pattern of threes . . . we knit . . .
God, the Son, the Holy Spirit.
Elizabeth, Mary, Martha . . .
Women of faith who have led the way.

Melodies quiet the soul and dismiss all stress,
As we knit.
The knitting continues and becomes a shawl
To be a wrapping
Of love, compassion, and togetherness.

Embellished with fringe,
And blessed by the group.
It is presented as a token of care and concern,
Compassion or celebration.
Love embraces, encourages, sustains . . .
And the circle of love is complete.

"I was naked and you clothed me,
I was sick and you visited me . . .
As you did it to the least of these my brethren,
You did it unto me."

—MYRTLE L. COUNCIL
SHILLINGTON, PENNSYLVANIA

The Seven Sacraments

This story has significant meaning for me. Not only is the Reverend Deacon Francis B. Cole Jr. a deacon with Epiphany Catholic Cathedral, but he is also my father. Reading about his experience in receiving the Seven Sacraments has deepened my relationship with him and, along with the Prayer Shawl Ministry, has strengthened the bond between us. —Victoria A. Cole-Galo

By age 45 I had received all Seven Sacraments. Now, at 75, the blessings and commitments that each of the sacraments imparted have led me to reflect on this journey of life.

Baptism

My first journey to church occurred 1 month and 3 days after I was born. My parents were so very proud of me. I learned love from them and experienced the confidence they had in me. Baptism has been a major focus in the ministries that are open to me. During the twice-daily praying of liturgy of the hours, I pray for the 600-plus children I have had the privilege to baptize. Before the Shawl Ministry was started in our parish, we used a white bib or a small stole as the white garment in the liturgy. Now we are able to wrap the parents and child in a white prayer shawl as we pray over them with these words: "See in this white garment the outward sign of your Christian dignity." The white prayer shawl is warm, is comforting, and binds a family to their commitment to love and care for each other.

Reconciliation

I was very young when I made my first confession and have no recollection of this first encounter with a forgiving Lord. However, throughout the years, this sacrament has enriched my life with direction and focus as we seek forgiveness of any and all transgressions we experience. Our grandson made a prayer shawl for me, and I use it for comfort while praying and during my preparation for Reconciliation.

Eucharist

Holy Communion was my first step in my walk with Jesus, who is the strength in my life's journey. I recall inviting my best friend, John, to also walk with Jesus, and he followed my encouragement and made his First Communion. As young boys, we made plans to someday play football at Notre Dame. Our dreams ended when John committed suicide in his early teens. If only his parents could have wrapped themselves in a prayer shawl, it might have given them some comfort.

Confirmation

My first adult commitment to walk through life with Jesus Christ was at Confirmation. What I learned from caring parents came into focus as I grew and discerned the direction of my life. I also learned to live with dyslexia by focusing on the needs of others. Giving a prayer shawl for Confirmation can be a unique symbol of courage as one journeys into adult life.

Sacrament for the Sick and Dying

At age 17, my football career came to an end. I lay on a hospital bed with a severe injury to my knee, was prayed over, and received the Sacrament for the Sick just before a 10-hour operation that would allow me to continue to walk with both legs. Once more, I reflected on how John and I had to leave our plans to play football. The desire to continue my life started with my slow recovery, which also allowed me to be a big brother to John's younger brothers. It seemed that all the events and the richness of the sacraments directed me to caring and helping others. Now when I visit the sick and dying, I bring a prayer shawl with me to give comfort and peace.

Marriage

My relationship with my wife started on a rainy evening. I did not have to work as a lifeguard and instead attended a party, where I met the right person for me. It took 5 years to complete our education and responsibilities before we married. We had only 3 days for a honeymoon, so we committed the rest of our lives together as a continuous honeymoon. God blessed our commitment with four beautiful children, who have given us great joy and loving friendship. Our only daughter, Victoria, was inspired to

co-create the Prayer Shawl Ministry, and today it continues with us and with members of our family. When I officiate at a wedding, I present the bride and groom with a prayer shawl for their life journey.

Holy Orders

All of my life experiences have led me to a formal commitment to serve the Lord. As a part of the ritual of ordination to the Diaconate, we lay on the floor of the cathedral (as a sign of humility) while more than 2,000 people prayed the Litany of the Saints over us. When the moment came for me to rise, I heard the voice of my friend John, saying, "Get up and go forth into the world." The person speaking these words was actually the bishop, but the voice I heard was John's. "Receive the Gospel of Christ, whose herald you now are," he said. "Believe what you read, teach what you believe, and practice what you teach."

All Seven Sacraments have shaped and defined my life, allowing me to be a positive force for others. As a deacon, I see that the Prayer Shawl Ministry has brought an added dimension to my ministry. The marvel of this ministry is that prayer shawls have a place in all Seven Sacraments. God bless all those women and men who carry on what two inspired women have created!

REVEREND DEACON
FRANCIS B. COLE JR., Nokomis, Florida

PERFECT FOR A BEGINNER, THIS BASIC SHAWL IS ALL about increasing—and it's a good way to hone your technique if you haven't done so lately. The shawl starts with a small number of stitches, and one stitch is added at the beginning of each row, eventually growing into a full-size triangular shawl. The shawl can be worn as is, or finished off with a looped or standard fringe.

FROM
Susan Allgaier
Wixom, Michigan

BEAUTIFUL SHAWL

Skill Level
Easy

Finished Measurements
48 in long and 30 in deep

Yarn
• Approximately 250 yd bulky yarn
Shawl shown in Plymouth Apollo Thick and Thin (100% virgin wool; 95 yd/4 oz), 2 skeins #14 Wedgewood Blue

Needles
• Size 17 circular needle, 29 in long (or size needed to obtain gauge)
• Size K crochet hook (for optional looped fringe)

Gauge
• 8 sts and 10 rows = 4 in worked in Garter Stitch

DIRECTIONS
CO 9 sts (or number of your choice, up to 18 sts).

Row 1: Knit across.

Row 2: Inc 1 st, knit across. Repeat Row 2 until 110 sts are on needle. BO very loosely.

LOOPED FRINGE (optional)
With crochet hook, attach yarn to corner of one edge and ch 25. Anchor it to edge a few stitches down with a sl st. (**Note:** If this creates a loop too short for your liking, ch more sts until you get the effect you like.) Then continue down edge, attaching loops with evenly spaced sl sts.

FRINGE (optional)
Cut enough 14-in strands of yarn for desired fringe. Holding 2 to 4 strands tog, attach fringe every 1½ in, as shown on pp. 167–168. Tie beads or a charm into the fringe as desired.

KNOTS OF FAITH

Yarn woven with compassion
Purls of blessing,
Knots of faith,
Needles of strength.
Showing Your love,
A loop forever growing.
With one we are born,
Another we learn to trust.
Getting bigger, more elaborate.
Forever holding in Your endless love.
Forever holding out the pain
That would bring us from You.
Lord please bless the hands
That weave Your love.
Bless the needles
That hold us all together.
Bless the yarn
That loops our lives into one.
Lord bless the heart
That forever works in Your name.

—ALYSSA SCOTTI
BERLIN, CONNECTICUT

On My Rocking Chair

Inspired by an article in the *Hartford Courant*, I began a shawl ministry at the Unitarian Society of Hartford.

At the time, my elderly mother was slowly becoming less able to care for herself. We hired a wonderful woman, Alfreda, to care for her and provide some respite for my father. As I watched my mother slipping from us, I thought I would make her a shawl, something different from those that I had been knitting for our ministry. I used light blue yarn—one of my mother's favorite colors—to make a lacy triangular shawl. When I gave it to her, she commented on its soft feel. I hung it on the back of her favorite chair. When my mother died in April 2003, I gave her shawl to Alfreda as a thank-you gift for her gentle kindness.

As the months passed, I began to miss the shawl. I never regretted giving it to Alfreda, but I did wish that it could be in two places at once. I decided to reproduce it. When the shawl was complete, I hung it over my rocking chair, where I could always see it.

That might have been the end of my story. But some time later, a dear friend having a string of misfortunes seemed in need of a shawl. I took my shawl off the rocking chair and gave it to her. How bare the chair looked! I made yet another blue, lacy, triangular shawl to hang on the chair. I am happy to be able to share my blue, lacy triangles with friends or family members who need comfort. But I know I always need a blue, lacy triangle hanging on my rocking chair as a way to remember my mother.

VICKI CAREY, Bloomfield, Connecticut

CALMING SHAWL

JODI LEWANDA CHOSE THE BEE STITCH FOR HER SHAWL BECAUSE it is rhythmic and soothing. And she chose a serene color of the soft, spicy brown, curcuma and pale indigo. Paired with these natural cotton yarns, it makes for a very calming shawl to knit and to wear. A pocket attached on the underside of the shawl provides a place in which the giver or receiver could place a note, a charm, a prayer, a photo, or any other item that expresses the meaning of the wrap. For more information about adding symbols and charms to your shawl see Color and Symbology appendix on page 164.

Skill Level
Easy

Finished Measurements
56 in long and 20 in wide

Yarn
• Approx 550 yd each of two colors of worsted weight yarn (Colors A and B)
• Shawl shown in Nashua Handknits Natural Focus™ Ecologie Cotton (100% cotton; 110 yd/1.75 oz), 5 balls each #0083 Curcuma (Color A) and #0085 Indigo (Color B)

Needles
• Size 7 circular needle, 24 in or longer (or size needed to obtain gauge)
• Size G crochet hook

Notions
• Tapestry needle

Gauge
• 16 sts and 36 rows = 4 in worked in Bee Stitch

JODI LEWANDA'S
CALMING SHAWL

BEE STITCH
Row 1: With Color B, K1, *k1-b, k1* repeat from * to end.

Row 2: Knit.

Row 3: With Color A, K2, k1-b, *k1, k1-b*, repeat from * to last 2 sts, k2.

Row 4: Knit.

Repeat Rows 1–4 for pattern.

SHAWL
CO 81 sts in Color A.

Foundation Rows 1 and 2: Knit.

Work Bee Stitch until piece measures approx 56 in from CO edge, ending after Row 4.

With Color A, knit 1 row. BO.

EDGING
Row 1: With Color A and crochet hook, start at any corner and work 1 sc in each st along short edges and 1 sc in every other st (row ends) along long edges, making 3 sc in corners. Sl st to beginning sc. Fasten off.

Weave in ends. Lightly block.

POCKET
CO sts in Color B. Work in Stockinette Stitch (knit 1 row, purl 1 row) for 5 inches.

Work 3 rows of Garter Stitch (knit every row). BO.

Place pocket on inside of shawl approx 2 in from one short edge, centered between long edges. Sew in place with pocket opening (Garter Stitch end) toward middle of shawl.

THIS IS A PRAYER SHAWL

This is a prayer shawl;
Knitted with hymns,
Woven with prayers,
Created to soft melodies
And peaceful thoughts.
In the warmth of the shawl
May you feel God's comfort
And the spirit of healing,
In a time of need
Through the power of prayer.

—JANE ROBERTS
WEST CHESTER, PENNSYLVANIA

One of My Favorite Places

Everyone I know is rushing around, overbooked and juggling. I am no exception, and I need my daily planner book with me at all times. When the chance arose to contribute a pattern and model for this book, I jumped at the opportunity, but I had to check my calendar first to make sure I had time to produce the project. That's when the idea of making a calming shawl emerged. I needed to make a soothing item, a piece that would slow me down. I knew others would feel the same way.

As I started to plan my shawl, I thought it would be nice to make it in a fiber that would be suitable for everyone—something natural, not itchy, not too warm, almost like a gentle hug. That's how I chose Nashua Handknits Natural Focus Ecologie Cotton, with subtle color coming from natural plant dyes. The two colors I chose were Indigo (a very pale blue) and Curcuma (a soft neutral), and as I worked on the piece, I realized that the colors reminded me of water and sand—a quiet beach, one of my favorite places on earth.

Of all of my knitting, I most enjoy stitch work, and I set out to find a pattern that would complement both the yarn and the look of the completed shawl. I wanted to use a stitch that would be interesting yet not intricate and with a bit of texture; I settled on the Bee Stitch. As I progressed on the shawl, I found the stitch to be very rhythmic, and the weight of the cotton helped the stitches mold into one another. After just a few rows, I had learned the pattern well enough to just knit without thinking about the stitches. It was a very meditative and calming experience, just what I had hoped the project would be.

After the shawl reached the desired length, I was almost sorry to have to bind it off, but my "hug" was complete . . . well, almost. I decided to add a pocket on the inside, not just for decoration but for actual use. I thought it would be a perfect way to hold a note, a charm, or a written prayer as a reminder of the good thoughts that went into the shawl.

I would like to dedicate this shawl and its pattern to anyone who needs to stop running for a while, who needs to be introspective, who needs to just *be*. Designing and making this project gave me an excuse to be lost in my own thoughts, something I should do more often.

JODI LEWANDA, Farmington, Connecticut

C ABLES SYMBOLIZE UNITY AND MAY BE
used to celebrate weddings, commitments, or friendship.
This cable is made up of three sections to symbolize the lives of two individuals
and their relationship to God. Each section of the cable weaves together as each
individual's life is intertwined both with God and with one another.

FROM
Ruth Thompson
Gainesville, Georgia

REVERSIBLE CABLE SHAWL

Skill Level
Intermediate

Finished Measurements
60 in long and 18 in wide

Yarn
• Approx 675 yd bulky weight yarn
(**Note:** This shawl looks great without
fringe, but if fringe is desired, purchase
an additional 135–175 yd of yarn.)
Shawl shown in Lion Brand® Jiffy®
(100% acrylic; 135 yd/3 oz), 5 skeins
#450-134 Avocado

Needles
• Size 10 and 11 straight or circular needles
  (or size needed to obtain gauge)
• Cable needle

Gauge
• 20 sts and 18 rows = 4 in worked in
Cable Pattern

CABLE PATTERN
Row 1: Make first cable cross as follows:
Sl first st knitwise, p1, k1, p1 for side edge,
*sl next 4 sts onto cable needle and hold in
back of work, (k1, p1, k1, p1) over next 4 sts,
work sts from cable needle (k1, p1, k1, p1),
work next 4 sts (k1, p1, k1, p1), repeat from
* 5 more times, end (k1, p1, k1, p1) for
side edge.

Rows 2–4: Work in k1, p1 rib as
established, sl first st of each row.

Row 5: Make second cable cross as
follows: Sl first st knitwise, p1, k1, p1 for
side edge, *work (k1, p1, k1 p1) over next
4 sts, place next 4 sts on cable needle and
hold in front of work. Work next 4 sts
(k1, p1, k1, p1), work sts on cable needle
(k1, p1, k1, p1), repeat from * 5 more times,
end (k1, p1, k1, p1) for side edge.

Rows 6–8: Work in k1, p1 rib as
established, sl first st of each row.

DIRECTIONS

Note: To keep shawl edges even, sl first st of each row knitwise.

With smaller needles, CO 80 sts.

Sl first st of each row and work k1, p1 rib for 2 in.

While keeping k1, p1 rib as established, change to larger needles and begin Cable Pattern.

Repeat Rows 1–8 of Cable Pattern until shawl measures 58 in, or 2 in less than desired finished length. End with a cable cross row (Row 1 or Row 5).

Change to smaller needles and work 2 in. in k1, p1 rib as established, sl first st of each row. BO.

Block shawl to measure 18 in wide.

Blessed Union

When my friend Cindy invited me to officiate at her wedding ceremony, I was happy to say yes. As associate pastor, I had come to know Cindy through our church. Unfortunately, in the time leading up to her wedding date, Cindy had to undergo surgery followed by grueling medical treatments.

My husband and I began knitting a prayer shawl to celebrate the wedding. It was long enough to wrap around the couple. As we knitted, we prayed: "Knit them together in Your love, O God. Wrap them with the comfort of Your Christ. Weave the power of Your Spirit within them." We prayed for health for Cindy and strength for her fiancé, Michael.

The folded shawl, which held our prayers, was passed among the people in attendance, who all added their words of blessing. These community blessings transformed the traditional Christian service—the blessing of a civil marriage—into an open event. As we wrapped the prayer shawl around the couple for the final blessing, we wrapped them, too, in our love.

LUCY BRADY, Westminster, Maryland

FABRIC OF LIFE
(sung as a round)

*The fiber of my being, the fiber of your being,
the fiber of our being, the fiber of all being
Is spun into the yarn that binds us all and
knit into the fabric of life, all life.
We are interwoven, we are interwoven, we are
interwoven into the fabric of life.*

—LINDA SMITH KOEHLER
ORONO, MAINE

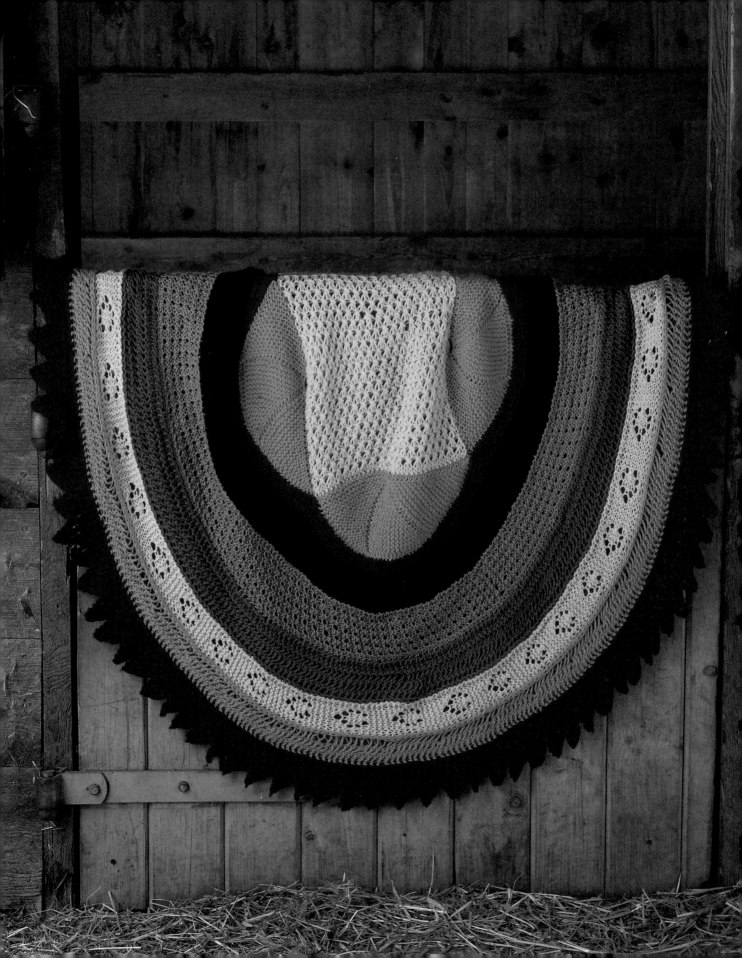

FROM
Ann Goodwin
Chapala, Jalisco, Mexico

DESIGNER ANN GOODWIN, WHO LIVES IN Mexico, writes: "One morning I saw a spectacular sunrise: yellow, orange, turquoise, mauve, and peach. It was so wonderful that I thought that I should try to capture it in a prayer shawl. How is it that I had all those colors in my stash of yarn?" In describing her shawl-knitting process, she says, "Each one evolves as I knit. . . . If I make a mistake, it becomes part of the design. Patterns repeat and end where they are supposed to. I do not have any control over what happens. Every shawl is first placed on the altar and given to God, and most of them have been blessed by a priest before being given further. The shawls are given as a ministry to anyone in a crisis. I have learned that many recipients immediately feel better as soon as they wrap the shawl around themselves."

We have paired this shawl with a touching story about three sisters from Colombia, South America. We like to envision a multicolored prayer shawl like this one providing comfort to a dying sister and enveloping a grieving family.

MEXICAN RAINBOW SHAWL

Skill Level
Experienced

Finished Measurements
Approx 56 in across

Yarn
• Approx 250 yd each of yellow, purple, blue, green, orange, and red sport weight yarn (or any 6 colors of your choice)
• Shawl shown in El Gato Meta (100% acrylic; 165 yd/1.75 oz), 2 skeins each of #04H Yellow, #22C Orange, #42C Red, #49M Purple, #65B Blue, and #95G Green

Needles
• Size 10½ straight or circular needles (or size needed to obtain gauge)

Notions
• Stitch markers

Gauge
• 30 sts and 26 rows = 4 in worked in Garter Stitch

MEXICAN RAINBOW SHAWL

DIRECTIONS

Note: Sl first st of every row purlwise, taking yarn around back and pulling tightly when knitting second st.

CENTER SQUARE

With Yellow, CO 40 sts. Knit 80 rows (40 ridges) of Garter Stitch (knit every row). BO loosely.

SEMICIRCLE ROUND

Work semicircles in Orange on each side of center square as follows:

With RS of square facing, pick up 19 sts (1 st per Garter Ridge) along one edge, starting at top right-hand corner (you will have 21 sts not picked up). Now work semicircle with short rows as follows:

First Segment: Row 1 (WS): Knit to end.

Row 2 (RS): Knit to last st, turn (yarn will be in front). Sl last st to left needle, wrap yarn around st to back, and replace st on right needle.

Row 3: K18, turn.

Row 4: Knit to last 2 sts, turn, wrap yarn as before around 2nd st from end.

Row 5: K17, turn.

Row 6: Knit to last 3 sts, turn, wrap yarn as before around 3rd st from end.

Row 7: K16, turn.

Continue to knit as established, knitting 1 less st each time, ending with k1, turn, wrap, k1.

Next 2 Rows: Knit across all sts. Right segment of arc is complete. Do not BO.

Second Segment: Next Row: Beginning with Row 2, repeat first segment. Center segment of arc is complete. Do not BO.

Third Segment: Next Row: Beginning with Row 2, repeat first segment. Left segment of arc is complete. Do not BO.

Join third segment of semicircle to center square by folding loose edge of semicircle to loose edge of center square with RS tog. BO tog (see p. 167) with WS of center square facing and working toward middle. There will be 2 sts left on center square, which match center arc of second segment of the semicircle.

Make 3 more Orange semicircles on other 3 sides of center square. Each semicircle should have 57 Garter Ridges, for a total of 228 ridges all around. Place a marker every 19 ridges. (These markers indicate inc rows.)

FIRST BAND—Garter Stitch

Note: Bands are attached as you knit around, as described.

With Red, pull 1 CO st through any bar between ridges of Orange semicircle; using Knitted Cast On (see p. 167), CO 6 more sts. (7 sts)

Row 1: K3, yo, k2tog, k1, knit last st tog with bar of Orange semicircle as follows: Sl last st knitwise, pull up a st in next bar of Orange edge, psso. Turn.

Row 2: Knit.

Repeat Rows 1 and 2 for pattern. Continue with

Red; inc at each marker by working twice into 1 bar of Orange edge. (Remember that when inc'ing around circle, you must work 2 extra rows—not sts—to make an inc.) To join first band, BO tog with CO edge. You should have 240 ridges in first band.

Place markers on edge of first band every 8 ridges, for incs in next band.

SECOND BAND—Faggoting Stitch
With Purple, pull 1 CO st through any bar between ridges of first band; using Knitted Cast On, CO 8 more sts. (9 sts)

Row 1 (RS): K8, sl last st knitwise, pull up a st in next bar of first band, psso. Turn.

Row 2 (WS): K3, (yo, sl 1 knitwise, k1, psso) 3 times.

Row 3: K1, (yo, sl 1 knitwise, k1, psso) 3 times, k1, sl 1, psso, pull up a st in next bar of first band, psso. Turn. (**Note:** The sl 1 is the yo of previous row.)

Repeat Rows 2 and 3 until round is complete; inc by working 2 rows into 1 bar at each marker. Move marker to outside edge of band as inc is made to mark inc row on next band. BO tog with CO edge.

THIRD BAND—Granite Stitch
(**Note:** Faggoting band has a ch st edge; pick up both loops when attaching third band.)

With Blue, pull 1 CO st through any bar between ridges of second band; using Knitted Cast On, CO 12 more sts. (13 sts)

continued

GREETINGS FROM YOUR PRAYER SHAWL

Hello! I am your Prayer Shawl.
Someone from your Prayer Shawl
Ministry group created me.
God's light shines through each hollowed
skein of yarn.
God's glory follows the yarn as it is
worked through their fingers,
into a beautiful, comfortable Prayer
Shawl.

. . . I was part of a rainbow of color,
from all the other shawls there that day.
Red tells you that Jesus gave his all to
rescue you.
Yellow is a sign of safety, and your faith
makes you strong.
Blue is a call to be true and honest, to
yourself and others.
If I am pink, you will feel comfort in
knowing the truth.
Green puts you at ease in new growth as
you prepare for the
newness-of-life walk.

Go and tell others this ministry of your
Prayer Shawl.
You need not but touch my fringe.
For Jesus hears and loves you.
Rejoice ever more. Thanks be to God.

—RUTH BEITELSPACHER
ABERDEEN, SOUTH DAKOTA

MEXICAN RAINBOW SHAWL

Row 1 (RS): K12, sl last st knitwise, pull up a st in next bar of second band, psso. Turn.

Row 2: Knit.

Row 3: K2, (k2tog) 5 times, attach as above, sl last st, pull up a st in next bar of second band, psso. (8 sts) Turn.

Row 4: K2, (knit into bar lying between last st and next st, k1) 5 times, k1. (13 sts)

Repeat Rows 1–4 until round is complete, inc by working 2 rows into 1 bar at each marker. Move marker to outside edge of band as inc is made to mark inc row on next band. BO tog with CO edge.

FOURTH BAND—Faggoting Stitch
With Green, repeat second band.

FIFTH BAND—Daisy Stitch
(**Note:** Faggoting band has a ch st edge; pick up both loops when attaching fifth band.)

With Yellow, pull 1 CO st through any bar between ridges of fourth band; using Knitted Cast On, CO 8 more sts. (9 sts)

Row 1 (RS): K8, sl last st knitwise, pull up a st in next bar of fourth band, psso. Turn.

Row 2 and all even rows: Knit.

Row 3: K4, yo, k2tog, sl last st, pull up a st in next bar of fourth band, psso. Turn.

Row 5: K2, k2tog, yo, k1, yo, k2tog, sl last st, pull up a st in next bar of fourth band, psso. Turn.

Rows 7 and 9: K1, k2tog, yo, k3, yo, k2tog,

sl last st, pull up a st in next bar of fourth band, psso. Turn.

Row 11: K3, yo, sl 2 tog knitwise, k1, pass 2 slipped sts over tog, yo, k3. Sl last st, pull up a st in next bar of fourth band, psso. Turn.

Rows 13–18: Knit.

Repeat Rows 1–18 until round is complete, inc by working 2 rows into 1 bar at each marker. Move marker to outside edge of band as inc is made to mark inc row on next band. BO tog with CO edge.

Note: As an alternative, work in Garter Stitch as for first band, inc by working 2 rows into 1 bar at each marker. Move marker to outside edge of band as inc is made to mark inc row on next band.

SIXTH BAND—Faggoting Stitch
With Orange, repeat second band.

BORDER—Triple Trinity Stitch
(**Note:** Faggoting band has a ch st edge; pick up both loops when attaching border.)

With Red, pull 1 CO st through any bar between ridges of first band; using Knitted Cast On, CO 6 more sts. (7 sts)
(**Note:** Do not sl first st at outside edge.)

Row 1 (RS): K2, yo, k1, yo, k1, yo, k4, sl last st knitwise, pull up a st in next bar of sixth band, psso. Turn.

Row 2 and all even rows: Knit.

Row 3: K2, yo, k2, yo, k2, yo, k3, sl last st, pull up a st in next bar of sixth band, psso. Turn.

Row 5: K2, yo, k3, yo, k3, yo, k4, sl last st, pull up a st in next bar of sixth band, psso. Turn.

Row 7: BO 9 sts, knit until 1 st remains, sl last st, pull up a st in next bar of sixth band, psso. Turn.

Row 8: Knit.

Repeat Rows 1–8 until round is complete, inc by working 2 rows into 1 bar at each marker, removing marker as inc is made. BO tog with CO edge.

Sew in ends and block.

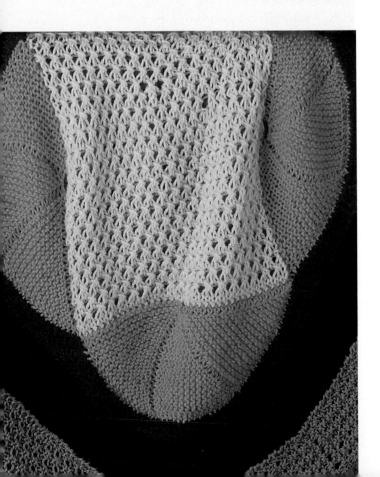

Three Sisters

As a chaplain at University of Iowa Hospitals, I see firsthand how giving prayer shawls to patients who are dying brings them comfort. One such patient is especially memorable.

Two sisters from Colombia had been sitting vigil beside their younger sister, 39-year-old Maria, who was dying from brain cancer. She was a striking woman with luxurious dark hair, partially shaved due to surgery. Still, she had a long black braid of hair that lay across her pillow. Maria's elderly parents lived in Colombia, and the sisters had been calling regularly to update them. They made the decision to stay in Colombia, being too fragile to travel. It was then that I thought of giving the family a prayer shawl.

I suggested that a prayer shawl could be something the sisters could send to their parents once Maria died. Both agreed. I brought in a purple prayer shawl and a multicolored one. Without hesitation, they chose the multicolored shawl.

The following Monday, I visited and was told that several friends had stopped by over the weekend and remarked how much the shawl was "just like Maria." "It is so soft," one sister said. Softness is needed during such harsh times, as is beauty. When life is so dark, beauty somehow helps balance the spirit; colors remind us that there is more, that healing of a different kind is possible.

After Maria died, the sisters sent the shawl to their parents in Colombia—a reminder of their soft and beautiful daughter's final journey.

MARY KAY KUSNER, Iowa City, Iowa

LACY LINEN STOLE

THIS SHAWL IS CLEVERLY DESIGNED WITH A TWO-SIDED cable pattern—no matter which side of the shawl is facing out, the fabric looks finished and lovely. The original is knit in a 100% linen yarn, which drapes beautifully and is surprisingly easy to care for—it can simply be machine washed and dried, which also makes it softer over time. Trudy Van Stralen offers a lovely thought to meditate on as you work this pattern: "The cables in this shawl remind me of gentle, stretchable ropes, holding the world softly together, so we can all live within those boundaries in peace."

Skill Level
Intermediate

Finished Measurements
63 in long and 16½ in wide

Yarn
- Approx 700 yd sport weight yarn
- Shawl shown in Euroflax Fine Sport Weight (100% linen; 270 yd/3.5 oz), 3 skeins #52 Grape

Needles
- Size 7 straight needles (or size needed to obtain gauge)
- Size F crochet hook
- Cable needle

Gauge
- 20 sts and 24 rows = 4 in worked in Cable Pattern

Note: If you are using Euroflax linen, you must machine wash and dry your sample before measuring gauge. An exact gauge is not critical.

CABLE
Sl next 3 sts onto cable needle, hold at front of work, k3, k3 from cable needle (3/3LC)

DIRECTIONS
CO 82 sts. Begin Cable Pattern as follows:

Row 1: P2, (k6, p6) 6 times, k6, p2.

Row 2: K2, (p6, k6) 6 times, p6, k2.

Row 3: P2, (3/3LC, p6) 6 times, 3/3LC, p2.

Row 4: Repeat Row 2.

Row 5: Repeat Row 1.

Row 6: Repeat Row 2.

Row 7: Repeat Row 1.

Row 8: K2, (p6, 3/3LC) 6 times, p6, k2.

Row 9: Repeat Row 1.

Row 10: Repeat Row 2.

Row 11: Repeat Row 1.

Row 12: Repeat Row 2.

Work 12-row Cable Pattern a total of 30 times. Work Rows 1–4 once more. BO loosely knitwise.

FINISHING
Using crochet hook, work reverse sc (see p. 167) around entire edge of stole.

Machine wash stole on a gentle cycle using a nonbleach mild soap. Tumble dry on medium heat. Press with steam iron, if desired.

PRAYER OF GATHERING

God of Life, God of Love, God of Compassion,

We give You thanks for the gathering of our knitting group. We give You thanks for the shawls we create. We give You thanks for each other and all those for whom we knit.

Bless, O God, our time together. Bless our hearts that they might be filled with Your spirit. Bless our hands that they might be touched by Your creative power. Bless our knitting that the shawls may be filled with Your love. Breathe in us the gift of Your grace so that our hearts may be Your heart, our hands may be Your hands, and our work may be Your work, now and forevermore. Amen.

—PATSY BROWN
NEWBURY, MASSACHUSETTS

FROM
Marian McKittrick
Versailles, Indiana

This shawl uses blocks of seven rows of seven stitches separated by three rows and three stitches, symbolic of the Trinity. Seven is symbolic of completion and perfection—God rested on the seventh day of Creation. The number seven is used throughout the Bible, especially in John and Revelation. Many shawls, as we have mentioned, focus on groupings of stitches. If this is of less interest to you, you will still want to try the pattern. Like its name, this dependable design will be one that you'll come back to when looking for a warm and beautifully textured shawl.

CORNERSTONE SHAWL

Skill Level
Easy

Finished Measurements
62 in long and 21 in wide

Yarn
- Approx 700 yd worsted weight yarn
- Shawl shown in TLC Heathers (100% acrylic; 260 yd/5 oz), 3 skeins #2445 Smoke Green

Needles
- Size 15 straight needles
- Size 13 straight needles (or size to obtain gauge)

Gauge
- 18 sts and 24 rows = 4 in worked in pattern using smaller needles

CORNERSTONE SHAWL

DIRECTIONS

With larger needles, CO 53 sts. Switch to smaller needles to work pattern.

Rows 1–7: *(P1, k1), repeat from * across row.

Row 8: K1, p1, (k9, p1) 5 times, p1, k1.

Row 9: *K1, p1, k1, (p7, k1, p1, k1), repeat from * across row.

Rows 10–12: *K1, (p1, k1), repeat from * across row.

Repeat Rows 8–12 for a total of 14 pattern repeats.

Last 2 Rows: *K1, (p1, k1), repeat from * across row.

BO in pattern.

NO FARTHER THAN A PRAYER

I wrap the prayers of warmth and love around your weary frame, praising, thanking God for the gift of you as I pray your name.

Every stitch sends forth a plea that joy will fill your soul. On and on the needles fly, making a pattern of prayer gold.

The shawl takes on a holiness for prayer is wrapped inside. It is so soft and warm, a place where you can hide.

It becomes a prayer itself, this pain that you endure. And it rises with love's incense, sacred, warm, and sure.

So as you wrap the shawl around may you feel my presence there. I may not sit beside you but I am no farther than a prayer.

Peace and love

—JEAN QUIGLEY
REHOBOTH, MASSACHUSETTS

Praying Voices

The Prayer Shawl Ministry is a life-altering path I have chosen . . . or did it choose me? Two years ago, at a knitting friend's suggestion, I decided to join First Church in Longmeadow's prayer shawl group, even though I was the only one who wasn't a church member. At the time, my daughter was serving her second tour of duty in Iraq. This weighed heavily on my mind, and being at a loss over world events and how they affected my family, I passionately wanted to make prayer shawls for our wounded soldiers.

My path had been chosen, but I had no idea the power of passion I would encounter. I called the Walter Reed hospital, where Chaplain John Kallerson agreed to accept the prayer shawls. Next, using the Prayer Shawl Ministry website's national database, I contacted approximately 80 prayer shawl groups, suggesting they consider sending prayer shawls to Walter Reed for our wounded soldiers. A few months later, Chaplain Kallerson told me he was receiving an average of 100 shawls weekly. They never sat in his office for more than a few days before he'd pile them onto a cart and cheerfully hand them out to soldiers on the hospital floor.

Not long ago, I heard an astonishing story, shared by a prayer shawl knitter: Her friend, a Franciscan brother, encountered a young Walter Reed patient with a prayer shawl wrapped around his shoulders. When the monk asked the soldier what it was, the soldier replied that he wasn't sure, but that it had just been given to him and he enjoyed the shawl's warmth. Then the soldier paused and said that when he wore it, he could hear praying voices. Hearing that story, I realized the Divine presence in our knitted gifts.

My passion to make prayer shawls for our wounded soldiers continues as I seek ways to send shawls to families whose children did not make it home. After months of roadblocks, I have found help from my state senator, Ted Kennedy. He connected me with a division of the Army that provided me with the names of fallen soldiers' families willing to accept gifts. With this new inspiration, I set up a website (home. earthlink.net/~ps4fs/shawls) in anticipation that my passion for these divine knitted shawls will bring even more hope, love, and peace.

COZETTE HAGGERTY, Wilbraham, Massachusetts

FROM
Victoria A. Cole-Galo
& Rosann Guzauckas
Wethersfield, Connecticut

WE SUGGEST THIS PATTERN FOR FIRST-TIME knitters—it's made with knit stitches only, known as the Garter Stitch. The same effect can be achieved with all purl stitches, too—a fun way to master the purl stitch if it's new to you. Once you are comfortable with either stitch, you're ready to begin making a prayer shawl. Also, several shawl makers have told us they made their first shawl for someone who has or had cancer. The shawl pictured here was made in pink—the symbolic color of breast cancer survivors.

BEGINNER'S SHAWL

Skill Level
Easy

Finished Measurements
76 in long and 19 in wide

Yarn
- Approx 850 yd lightweight bouclé yarn
- Shawl shown in Jo-Ann™ Sensations™ Rainbow Bouclé (88% acrylic/13% nylon; 853 yd/11 oz), 1 skein Light Pink

Needles
- Size 10½ straight or circular needles (or size needed to obtain gauge)

Gauge
- 16 sts and 22 rows = 4 in worked in Garter Stitch

Note: This shawl can easily be made any size and with any yarn. When choosing yarn, refer to "Standard Yarn Weights," on p. 163. This will give you an indication of how much yarn you will need as well as what size needle. We recommend using large needles (size 10½ to size 15) and thick yarns for this type of shawl. You can use medium-weight yarns with large needles, too—the shawl will appear lacy. We do not recommend using small needles with thick yarn.

DIRECTIONS
CO 68 sts. Knit every row until shawl measures 76 in, or desired length. BO.

Light and Healing

On December 18, 2004, my 12-day-old grandson, Garrett James Denslaw, died. No words can describe this loss.

One day at my knitting group, a woman brought information about the Prayer Shawl Ministry. I read about it. Not long after, a close friend in the group presented me with a beautiful shawl.

At home, I wrapped my shawl around me and allowed myself to cry and grieve the loss of my grandson. Slowly, I sensed that healing was taking place within me. I hoped someday I would be able to knit prayer shawls for others who were hurting.

By August 2005, I was knitting prayer shawls. I always attach fringe, and sometimes I include a small silver heart charm.

Most of the shawls I knit are to offer comfort to people. Recently I began knitting shawls to celebrate the joys in life. Once the recipients wrap the shawl around themselves, they understand the meaning of the ministry.

As I look back, I can see that the Prayer Shawl Ministry provided direction, light, and healing on my journey of grief. This has been a true blessing in my life.

SUSAN ALLGAIER, Wixom, Michigan

IN WHOLENESS AND HEALTH

As this shawl is knit together with prayer, may your body and soul be again knit together in wholeness and health.

—THE REVEREND REBECCA SEGERS
PRESBYTERIAN CHURCH OF SWEET HOLLOW
MELVILLE, NEW YORK

FROM
Michael Zuravel
St. Petersburg, Florida

ALSO KNOWN HUMOROUSLY AS THE "HOLEY Trinity Shawl," this design features three lace sections running lengthwise. The lace rows involve three repeats of three eyelets, which are shifted over every other right-side row (although there really isn't a right or wrong side). Michael Zuravel, the designer, says, "I wanted the repetition to be mysterious. So, while the concept of the Trinity is there, it is not identifiable at first glance." This is a lacy pattern, but the shawl has nice body when knitted with a substantial worsted weight wool yarn. In addition, the crocheted fringe seems to be an extension of the body of the shawl, not simply added on.

MYSTERY OF THE TRINITY

Skill Level
Intermediate

Finished Measurements
60 in long and 22 in wide

Yarn
- Approx 800 yd worsted weight yarn
- Shawl shown in Plymouth Encore Colorspun (75% acrylic/25% wool, 200 yd/3.5 oz), 4 skeins #7009 (green/beige/gray)

Needles
- Size 10½ straight or circular needles
- Crochet hook, size J (optional)

Gauge
- 14 sts and 18 rows = 4 in worked in pattern.

MYSTERY OF THE TRINITY

DIRECTIONS
CO 79 sts.

Row 1 (RS): Sl 1 st purlwise with yarn in front, k9, *k2tog, yo, yo, k2tog, k2tog, yo, yo, k2tog, k2tog, yo, yo, k2tog, k9, repeat from * twice more, k6.

Row 2 (WS): Knit across (at double yo's, knit into the first yo, purl into the second yo).

Row 3: Slip 1 st purlwise with yarn in front, k14, *k2tog, yo, yo, k2tog, k2tog, yo, yo, k2tog, k2tog, yo, yo, k2tog, k9, repeat from * twice more, k1.

Row 4: Repeat Row 2.
Repeat Rows 1–4 until piece measures approx 60 in long. BO all sts.

CROCHET FRINGE (Optional)
With the crochet hook, pick up 1 st at the beginning of either the BO or CO edge and ch 10. Sc in each st in the ch. When you reach body of shawl, sc into next edge st. Then sc into the next edge st and create another 10-st ch. Repeat across entire edge, then repeat across the other edge.

MAY THIS SHAWL

Gracious and loving God,

May this shawl, knitted or crocheted with love and many prayers, bless the one receiving it.

*May that person feel the comfort, healing, peace, and love
of God the Father, Jesus the Son, and
the Holy Spirit knitted or crocheted into every stitch by a loving, praying person.*

*May the warmth it brings and the colors it bears soothe the body, heart, mind, and soul
of the wearer.*

Amen.

—JESSICA SIRIANO
BURKE, VIRGINIA

Surprise Shawl of Healing

My husband of 40 years died early one morning in May, leaving a void in my life that I didn't know how to fill. I found myself trying to find something to do, because I had done so much for him for so long. That September, I came across the Prayer Shawl Ministry. I just could not stop reading about it. I knew that there was a reason for this; I prayed about it and felt like it was something I must look into more. A couple of Sundays later, the pastor preached a sermon from Isaiah 41:10—"Fear thou not, I will help thee"—that seemed meant for me. He said that God was asking us to put Him to the test. He would not let us down. Just try Him.

I told God that day I *would* put Him to the test; I would start a Prayer Shawl Ministry and trust that He would help me, even though I had not done any knitting in years. Within an hour of my making this commitment, I heard about a young lady who was very sick, and it seemed that she was not going to recover. I began to make her a shawl.

Meanwhile, this young lady attended a service at a church that had a shawl ministry, and in their services they used some shawls that had been blessed in the holy land of Israel. They had prayed for her healing and wrapped a shawl around her, and she said that, as they did, she could feel something special coming through. When the service was over, she had felt sad because she could not bring the shawl home with her.

I prayed for her as I worked on her shawl, and when it was completed, I printed out a prayer for her. I sent the shawl to her through a neighbor, and what a blessing I received from this. The young woman called me in tears and thanked me over and over for the prayer shawl. I still continue to pray for her even though she is healed now, much to the doctors' surprise. They cannot explain how her illness is no longer showing up on the tests and scans. We, however, know that God is still in control, and though the shawl has no magical healing powers, it does give her a constant reminder of where healing begins and ends.

NADINE JONES, Meadville, Mississippi

TUMBLING BLOCK STOLE

THIS STOLE IS KNIT IN SOOTHING, NURTURING SHADES of pink—a visual prayer for the user to be in the pink of health," says Kaffe Fassett, designer of this stole. The shawl is knit with two yarns held together—one a DK weight wool in vibrant colors, the other a lightweight blend of silk and mohair, which adds a smooth feel and extra warmth. The tumbling block design is one of Kaffe's classic color patterns and is enjoyable to knit. Mix and match colors as you desire to create the colored stripes and tumbling block pattern. The original combines 6 colors of mohair and 5 colors of DK yarn to create 17 different shades!

Skill Level
Experienced

Finished Measurements
60 in long and 28½ in wide

Yarn
- Approx 200 yd lightweight mohair in each of 6 colors
- Approx 250 yd DK weight yarn in each of 5 colors
- Shawl shown in Rowan Kidsilk Haze (70% kid mohair/ 30% silk; 229 yd/0.085 oz); 1 skein each of #606 Candy Girl, #596 Marmalade, #592 Heavenly, #583 Blushes, #600 Dewberry, and #630 Fondant; and Rowan Scottish Tweed (100% wool; 123 yd/1.75 oz); 2 skeins each of #11 Sunset, #10 Brilliant Pink, #05 Lavender, #03 Skye, and #24 Porridge

Needles
- Size 8 straight or circular needles (or size needed to obtain gauge)

Gauge
- 14 sts and 20 rows = 4 in worked in Stockinette Stitch with 1 strand DK yarn and 1 strand lightweight mohair held tog

Note: Entire shawl is worked with 1 strand of DK yarn and 1 strand of lightweight mohair held tog.

The way is not in the sky.
The way is in the heart.

—BUDDHA

TUMBLING BLOCK STOLE

STRIPED BORDER 1
CO 100 sts.

Using 1 strand each of DK yarn and mohair in colors of choice, work 4 rows in Garter Stitch (knit every row). The next row will be a RS row.

*Change color(s) and work 5 rows in Stockinette Stitch (knit 1 row, purl 1 row). Repeat from * 3 times (4 stripes total). The next row will be a WS row.

Change color(s) and work 1 row. The next row will be a RS row.

TUMBLING BLOCKS BORDER 1
Beginning with a RS row and colors of choice, follow chart. When chart is complete, work 1 row in Stockinette Stitch in color of choice.

STRIPED BODY
Continue as for striped border, working in Stockinette Stitch and changing color(s) every 5 rows, as desired, for a total of 38 stripes (or desired number—fewer for a shorter shawl and more for a longer shawl). End with 1 row of Stockinette Stitch in the same color as the single row ending the first tumbling blocks border.

TUMBLING BLOCKS BORDER 2
Following chart, work tumbling blocks border, using colors to repeat the first tumbling blocks border mirror-wise. End with 1 row of Stockinette Stitch in the same color as the single row ending the first striped border.

STRIPED BORDER 2
Repeat the first striped border, reversing the order of the stripe colors or choosing new colors, if desired. End with 4 rows of Garter Stitch in color of choice.

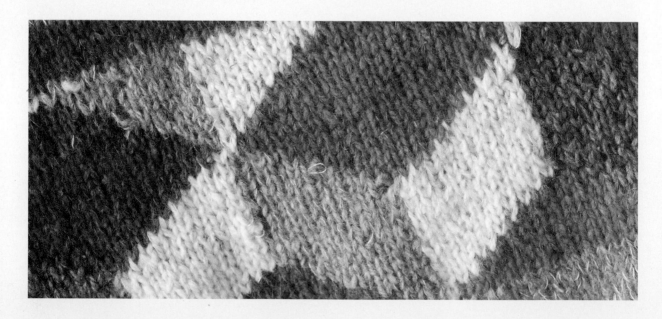

Tumbling Block Chart

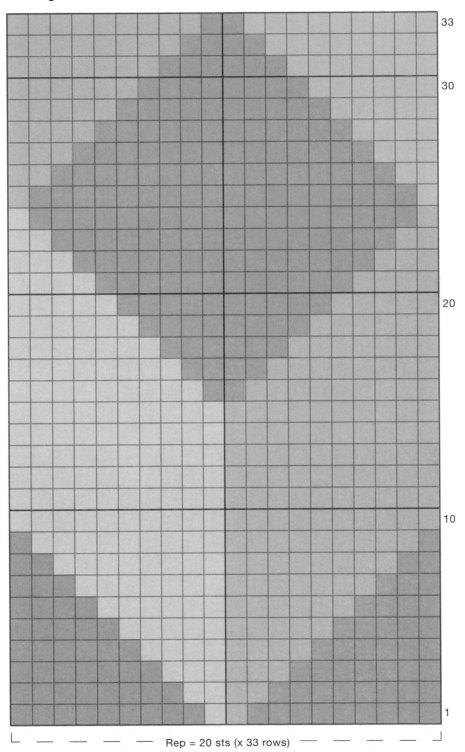

33

30

20

10

1

Rep = 20 sts (x 33 rows)

THIS LOVELY SHAWL USES MOSAIC KNITTING to create a color pattern, including three butterflies on each end of the shawl. Esther Paris, the designer of this shawl, writes, "The butterfly was my very first stab at picture knitting *ever*. I locked myself in the car at a vacant parking lot and taught myself to mosaic knit. This way no one would bug me while I learned something new and challenging." Once she had the technique down, she designed this unique shawl. Esther calls this design a "grief shawl." As you, too, master this technique, think of the butterflies as lifting the spirits of a bereaved recipient with their gentle, graceful wings.

FROM
Esther A. Paris
Cumberland, Rhode Island

BUTTERFLIES IN THREES

Skill Level
Experienced

Finished Measurements
58 in long and 15 in wide

Yarn
- Approx 400 yd worsted weight yarn in Background Color and 300 yd worsted weight yarn in Picture Color
- Shawl shown in Lion Brand Pound of Love (100% acrylic; 1,020 yd/16 oz), 1 skein each #550-099 Antique White (Background Color) and #550-110 Denim (Picture Color)

Needles
- Size 8 straight or circular needles (or size needed to obtain gauge)

Gauge
- 20 sts and 20 rows = 4 in worked in charted pattern

BUTTERFLIES IN THREES

Notes on Mosaic Knitting

- Read chart from right to left *only*.

- Every other RS row is worked in one color; alternate RS rows are worked in other color.

- WS rows are worked in same color as RS row previously worked—that is, Rows 1, 2, 5, and 6 are all worked in Background Color. Rows 3, 4, 7, and 8 are all worked in Picture Color. WS rows are *not* pictured on charts.

- When working RS rows, knit only those sts to be done in that row's color (represented by salmon colored boxes in the chart) and sl rest.

- When working corresponding WS rows, work only sts knit on previous row and sl rest.

- Chart indicates which sts are to be worked in which color. Row color indicates which yarn is being used at a time—for example, if you are working a Background Color row, all Picture Color sts are slipped; if you are working a Picture Color row, all Background Color sts are slipped.

- Be sure any yarn "floats" stay on WS of work.

- For more instruction on mosaic knitting, see *A Fourth Treasury of Knitting Patterns,* by Barbara G. Walker, and *Slip Stitch Knitting: Color Pattern the Easy Way,* by Roxana Bartlett.

FIRST SET OF BUTTERFLIES

CO 74 sts in Background Color. Knit 10 rows.

Add Picture Color.

Row 1: Following Row 1 of chart for Garter Stitch Borders (p. 74) from right to left and bottom to top, work Garter Stitch edge once, knitting Picture Color at Xs and slipping Background Color sts otherwise. Change to Butterfly Chart and repeat Row 1 of Butterfly Chart 3 times across row, following chart from right to left and bottom to top. Work other Garter Stitch edge once.

Row 2: Knit Picture Color on Garter Stitch edge and sl Background Color sts. Purl Picture Color sts for butterflies and sl Background Color sts. Knit Picture Color sts in second Garter Stitch edge and sl Background Color sts.

Row 3: Working with Background Color and following Row 3 of both charts, knit Background Color sts and sl Picture Color sts across first Garter Stitch edge, butterflies, and second Garter Stitch edge.

Row 4: Working back with Background Color, knit Background Color sts in Garter Stitch edges. Sl Picture Color sts. Purl Background Color sts across butterflies. Sl Picture Color sts across butterflies. Work Garter Stitch edge as before.

Repeat Rows 1–4 until entire Butterfly Chart is completed, ending with Row 48 (the WS of Row 47).

continued

Butterfly Chart

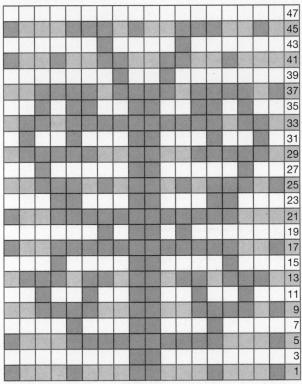

Work Butterfly Chart in Stockinette Stitch. Repeat 3 times across shawl center's width. Follow chart from bottom to top. Salmon colored boxes represent picture color stitches. Blank cells represent Background Color stitches.

☐ and ☐ Background Color Row
☐ Picture Color Row

PRAYER OF COMFORT

*May this prayer shawl surround
you with the Love of God.
May you feel the embrace of God,
who though unseen, is with you now.
May you be shielded from all that
causes you worry and anxiety.
Rest in the knowledge that you are
loved and cared for by a God
Whose gentle touch caresses your soul.*

*May you be strengthened by the prayers
of those who knit this shawl.
Though they do not know you personally,
It is their intention to bring you comfort
through the symbol of this shawl.
Together, they join with you
in the hope that
Your journey will be more peaceful.*

*May this prayer shawl be of
comfort to your family also.
May they draw courage from its beauty,
Trusting that when they are not
able to be here,
God remains and is present with you.*

*May God bless you with
love beyond measure.
May God's face shine upon you
and give you peace.*

Amen.

—MARY KAY KUSNER
IOWA CITY, IOWA

BODY OF SHAWL

Keeping shawl edges in Garter Stitch pattern as established, change to chart for body of shawl (again reading chart from right to left and bottom to top) and continue knitting and slipping sts as established. Continue until shawl measures approx 46 in, or 12 in less than desired length.

Body Chart

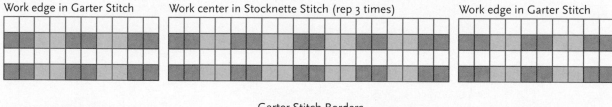

Work edge in Garter Stitch · Work center in Stocknette Stitch (rep 3 times) · Work edge in Garter Stitch

SECOND SET OF BUTTERFLIES

Keeping shawl edges in Garter Stitch pattern as established, change to Butterfly Chart. This time, you will work chart in reverse, working it from right to left as before but *from top to bottom* (beginning with Row 47 and ending with Row 1). This will reverse direction of butterflies on opposite end of shawl.

Garter Stitch Borders

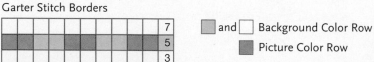

7
5
3
1

☐ and ☐ Background Color Row

■ Picture Color Row

After second set of three butterflies is completed, knit 10 rows in Background Color only. BO loosely. Block shawl if necessary.

Cyndee

Around the time when Victoria A. Cole-Galo and Janet Bristow were giving birth to the Prayer Shawl Ministry, my friend Cyndee was diagnosed with breast cancer. Janet started a shawl for her. She brought the beginnings of the mantle to our weekly prayer meeting and gave it to me. I began to knit, then passed the shawl around for other members to work on and pray over. I continued to work on the shawl everywhere I went—in meetings, in waiting rooms, at a concert, in the car. I added an angel to the fringe, prayed over the shawl, and called on all the women who have gone before us to watch over my dear friend as she traveled along this difficult road.

I couldn't wait to give Cyndee the prayer shawl when I went to visit her in Chicago. Tears streaming down her face, she wrapped herself up in it and said she could feel the love that was knitted into it.

When she started her chemotherapy, the mantle I gave her went with her. In that frigid room, waiting to have her treatment, she wrapped herself up in her shawl to feel warm, safe, and loved. Well, everyone who entered the room asked about the prayer shawl, and she was happy to tell them about it. Nurses began requesting shawls for other cancer patients. Cyndee knit two or three a week, bringing them along with her when she went for chemo. After finishing her treatment, she continued to bring shawls every week.

Two years ago, Cyndee and her husband, Joe, moved to Florida. During a visit to Connecticut, she told me she feared something was wrong. It turned out that her cancer had come back with a vengeance after nearly 9 years. When I went to her in Florida, she was very sick. I found her in her hospital bed, wrapped up in her prayer shawl. Saying good-bye that time was extremely painful. I knew it was probably the last time I would see my best friend of 30 years. It was.

Afterward, I received a box in the mail from Joe, who has kept up the ministry Cyndee started. It held a letter and the shawl I'd knit for Cyndee. "Eight years ago you gave me the gift of a lifetime," she wrote. "It eased my pain and suffering, and it has always given me a feeling of hope no matter what happens. With your loving gift I knew I would always be wrapped in the wings of angels. Take this mantle and wrap yourself in it whenever you miss me. I'll be there with you." I did and still do.

GINNY OWENS, Farmington, Connecticut

PATCHWORK SHAWL

MARILYN WEBSTER'S PRAYER SHAWL **SYMBOLIZES** many things: perseverance, grief, hope, even celebration. Knit with a luxurious yarn and meditative patterns— the Seed Stitch and the Wheat Stitch—the shawl is as healing to knit as it is to wear.

Skill Level
Intermediate

Finished Measurements
60 in long and 25 in wide

Yarn
- Approx 1,000 yd worsted weight yarn
- Shawl shown in Alchemy Yarns Synchronicity (50% silk/50% Merino wool; 110 yd/1.75 oz), 10 skeins #75M Champagne

Needles
- Size 10 circular needles, at least 29 in long (or size needed to obtain gauge)

Gauge
- 18 sts and 20 rows = 4 in worked in Patchwork Pattern

DIRECTIONS
CO on 269 sts.

Work Rows 1–8 of Patchwork Pattern chart.

Repeat Rows 9–36 four times.

Work Rows 37–43.

BO in pattern.

MARILYN WEBSTER'S
PATCHWORK SHAWL

Key

☐ Knit on RS, purl on WS

• Purl on RS, knit on WS

☐ Knit into st below (insert needle into st below next st on left needle and knit it in the usual way, slipping the st above off needle at the same time.)

kfk Knit front, knit (with right needle in front of left needle, skip the 1st st on left needle and knit the 2nd st through the front loop, then knit the skipped st and slip both off left needle.)

kbk Knit back, knit (with right needle behind left needle, skip the 1st st on left needle and knit the 2nd st through the back loop, then knit the skipped st through the front loop and slip both off left needle.)

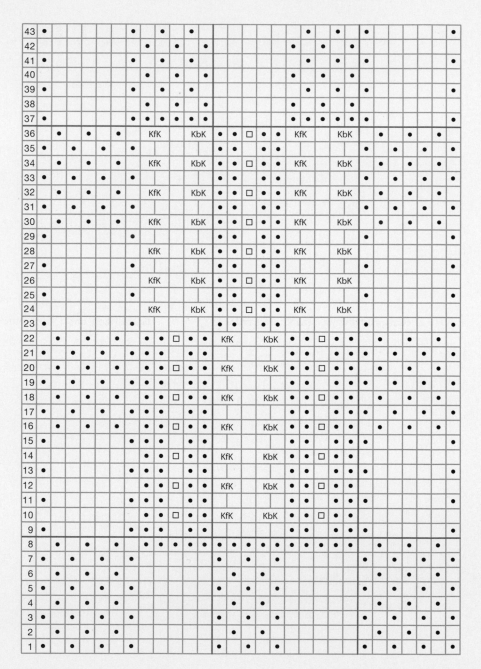

How to Pray?

When my sister was diagnosed with leukemia, the network of prayer spread around the world in an ever-widening web of family, friends, and friends of friends—all with different faiths and religious traditions, each praying in her or his own way. I, however, was not sure how to pray. As a young child, I believed there was a right way to pray and was convinced that my prayers were not worthy enough for God. As a teenager, desperate to unravel the mysteries of prayer, someone taught me to use the word *pray* as an acronym for praise, repent, ask, yourself. As an adult, certain of the power of prayer but still stuck with my childhood notions, I just stopped trying.

I may not know how to pray, but I know how to be quiet and knit. I knit to create beauty, to give gifts, to curb my anxiety, and to let my thoughts wander. During her illness, I knit my sister hats and head scarves, finishing the first one the day she asked her nurse to shave off her remaining hair. I knit while she slept. I knit while we chatted. I knit while she was out of the room for yet another procedure. I knit while we waited at the outpatient clinic for transfusions of blood and platelets. I knit alone at home. And when my sister expressed a desire to knit, too, I brought her yarn and needles from my stash, and we knit together.

After my sister died, it was hard to knit and even harder to pray. Then on a night in early spring, I sat in an armchair listening to music and picked up my needles to knit this shawl. The music, "Healing Chant to the Mother of Us All" (on *ReTurning*, by Jennifer Berezan with Linda Tillery and Sharon Burch, Edge of Wonder Records, 2000), was the piece my sister chose for her memorial service. The shawl was a simple, repetitive pattern that let me relax into the knitting. The stitches, Seed Stitch and Wheat Stitch, suggest growth and nourishment. The yarn, soft and luscious, offers comfort. The color, champagne, evokes celebration. Alone with this music and the rhythm of my knitting, I felt a deep peace. Perhaps this is prayer.

MARILYN WEBSTER, Forestville, California

THE PURSE STITCH CREATES A PATTERN THAT looks much like latticework. The shawl shown here was knit with size 15 needles with worsted weight yarn, creating a lacy look. Experiment with different weight yarns and smaller needles for a tighter pattern. The fringe is crochet chains; alternating loops of long chains and short chains make for a staggered effect.

FROM
Julie Dietz
Sigel, Illinois

LATTICE SHAWL

Skill Level
Intermediate

Finished Measurements
57 in long and 28 in wide, excluding fringe

Yarn
- Approx 600 yd worsted weight yarn
- Shawl shown in bulky 100% acrylic yarn

Needles
- Size 15 straight or circular needles (or size needed to obtain gauge)
- Size J crochet hook

Gauge
- 8 sts and 14 rows = 4 in worked in Garter Stitch

DIRECTIONS
CO 60 sts (or any multiple of 2 + 1 st on each end for selvedge sts).
Note: On every row, sl first st as if to purl with yarn in front. Take yarn to back, then work rest of the row as per pattern.

Rows 1–10: Sl 1 st, knit across row.

Row 11: Sl 1 st, k4, *yo, p2tog, repeat from * until 5 sts remain, k5.

Repeat Row 11 until shawl measures 55 in, or 1–2 in from desired length.

Next Row: Sl 1 st, knit across row. Repeat 9 times, for a total of 10 rows (to match beginning); BO.

CROCHET FRINGE
With crochet hook, attach yarn to right-hand edge of one end of shawl. *Ch 30, sk 3 sts, sc, ch 15, sk 3 sts, sc, repeat from * across end of shawl. Fasten off. Repeat on opposite end of shawl.

Iris and Lily

Our pastor officiated at a funeral for a lady who had a beautiful garden filled with irises and lilies. She had loved those flowers, and it was mentioned in the service that she would be tending to them in heaven. As these words were spoken, a woman began to sob loudly.

Afterward, a gentleman came up to the pastor and apologized for his wife, who had broken down. He explained that their daughter had recently given birth to premature twin girls—Iris and Lily. Iris was still in critical condition, but Lily had passed away. Our pastor gave the man and his wife, the twins' grandparents, a baby shawl that had been made by our Prayer Shawl Ministry, explaining the intent of the shawl ministry as he did. The babies' grandmother just hugged the shawl. She said that it was the color of the babies' nursery, and that they would take it to the hospital that afternoon. She was very, very touched, as were the babies' parents.

The shawl remained either in or over Iris's incubator for the remainder of her hospital stay. Three months later, baby Iris went home with none of the complications that most premature babies face—a miracle, considering that she weighed less than 2 pounds at birth. In the note they sent to our church after receiving the prayer shawl, Iris's parents said the shawl had been a huge source of strength and comfort to them. In our Prayer Shawl Ministry, we like to think of this as a "ripple effect"—the blessings flow from the person making the shawl, to the person receiving it, to the people who hear the stories, and on and on.

JANIE RUPRIGHT, Fort Wayne, Indiana

EVERY LOVINGLY CRAFTED STITCH

Every lovingly crafted stitch contains
a special prayer—
That God will send His peace to you
and keep you in His care.

As the shawl drapes 'round your
shoulders in morning or at night,
Know that He is with you always to
make your burden light.

—LINDA M. MULDOON
BRAINTREE, MASSACHUSETTS

TWO HEART WARMERS

WREN ROSS OFFERS TWO VERSIONS OF A DESIGN she calls a "heart warmer"—a shrug-like garment that is particularly comforting for women who have undergone a mastectomy. The Seed Stitch used in this pattern allows the knitter to meditate on each stitch as a seed of hope, which takes time, persistence, and love to grow.

Seeds of Intention Heart Warmer

Skill Level
Easy

Size
Small, Medium, Large

Finished Measurements
13⅓ (13¾, 14⅓ in long by 42 (45, 48) in wide

Yarn
• Approx 175 yd. super bulky yarn
• Shawl shown in Rowan Big Wool Fusion (100% merino wool, 87 yd/3.5 oz), 2 skeins #003 Cyclamen

Needles
• Size 17 straight or circular needles (or size needed to obtain gauge)

Notions
• Button, approx. 1 in

Gauge
• 8 sts and 14 rows = 4 in worked in Seed Stitch

DIRECTIONS
CO 9 sts.

Rows 1–4: Knit.

Row 5–6: Kf&b, k2, work Seed Stitch (k1, p1 across) until last 3 sts, k2, kf&b.

Repeat Rows 5–6, continuing to kf&b in the first and last st of each row, and maintaining Seed Stitch by knitting the purl sts and purling the knit sts as they face you, until you have 87 (93, 99) sts or piece measures 13 (13⅓, 14) in. from CO. Repeat Rows 1–4. BO loosely.

FINISHING
Tack left front over right front to form V neck. Sew button to center, below the V.

WREN ROSS'S
TWO HEART WARMERS

Garter Stitch Heart Warmer

Skill Level
Easy

Size
One size fits most. To make it smaller, work fewer rows. To make it larger, work more rows.

Finished Measurements
13 in long by 48 in wide.

Yarn
- Approx 135 yd super bulky yarn
- Shawl shown in Rowan Biggy Print (100% merino wool, 33 yd/3.5 oz), 4 skeins #261 Pool Party

Needles
- Size 19 straight or circular needles (or size needed to obtain gauge)

Notions
- Button, approx. 1 in

Gauge
- 5½ sts and 7 rows = 4 in worked in Garter Stitch

DIRECTIONS
CO 16 sts.

Row 1: Kf&b, knit to last st, kf&b.

Repeat Row 1 for 37 times, until you have 90 sts or piece measures 12 in from CO or desired length.

BO loosely.

FINISHING
Tack left front over right front to form V neck. Sew button to center of V.

Beauty Is My Medicine

I could never be an ascetic and renounce all worldly goods. Pretty things are too important to me. Sure, it's loftier to rise above materialism and vanity, but I must admit that my mood can lift radically just by looking at the intricacies of a favorite ring, watching a fuchsia sunset, or getting a good haircut. Beauty is my medicine.

My friend Krista Weller also felt this way when, at 32, she was diagnosed with breast cancer. The day Krista got the news a friend sent her an essay about *hózhó*, which is the Navaho belief that beauty, balance, order, and harmony are essential components of life.

"Why should I feel any less beautiful now than I did before?" Krista thought. "It's not about vanity as much as not wanting to feel different. All women want to feel beautiful, inside and out, especially when facing the harsh reality of becoming a cancer patient."

As a cancer patient, she began to take on the look as well—scarves, hats, wigs, makeup to hide the green-gray tinge of her skin. And every time she used a scarf or a skullcap, she felt even more like a cancer patient. The items meant to camouflage her condition made her feel more isolated and exposed.

Her coping mechanism? Knitting. Each time she picked up her needles, she felt a sense of control, peace, and productivity. As time went by, she noticed more and more knitters among patients and caregivers in the hospital. Women would bide their time—waiting in line, waiting for doctors, waiting for their treatments to be over, waiting for their cancer to go away—by knitting or crocheting. A dedicated fashionista, Krista conceived a program to make women facing cancer treatment feel beautiful on the inside and out. Knit a Shrug—Give a Hug™ was born.

When Krista asked me to design a sample shrug for the program, my goal was to make a stylish wrap that would feel like an embrace without being confining. I wanted it to grace a woman's shoulders, cover her upper torso, and still reveal the curves of her body. I called it a "heart warmer" for two reasons: (1) It protects the heart chakra area and gives the wearer a sense of being cherished, and (2) I want the process of making the shrug to open the hearts of knitters so that they may cultivate their own personal qualities of kindness, hope, clarity, and love.

Years ago, I began a practice that I call "Seeds of Intention Knitting." This is a personal kind of knitting that allows me to listen to my inner thoughts and focus on what or whom I care about. I begin by washing my hands in order to transition from the daily grind to sacred quietude. Next, I light a candle to welcome inspiration. Then I take my yarn from its special embroidered bag, place a clean white cloth on my lap, and begin to knit seeds of positive intentions, affirmations, wishes, hopes, prayers, and gratitude into every stitch.

I like to think of the stitches in these patterns as seeds for hope that take time, persistence, and love to grow. This shrug is more than an accessory. It is an account of my time, meditations, and affirmations. It is a fabric filled with seeds of love—a tactile prayer.

The day I finished knitting Krista's Seeds of Intention Heart Warmer, I took a walk around my favorite pond. It was the first warm and brilliantly sunny day of spring. I stopped for a moment, dazzled by the shimmering splash of light reflecting like diamonds on the water, and I heard the gentle whisper of *hózhó,* reminding me to walk in beauty. I thought about Krista's journey with cancer and how her embrace of beauty helped heal her. I was filled with gratitude for the magnificence of nature and the power of pretty things to open our hearts so that there may be more room for love.

If you are interested in learning more about the Hugs of Hope Foundation and the Knit a Shrug—Give a Hug project, visit www.hugs-of-hope.org.

WREN ROSS, Boston, Massachusetts

PLANTING SEEDS OF INTENTION

May each stitch be a seed of beauty.
May each stitch be a seed of truth.
May each stitch be a seed of health.
May each stitch be a seed of compassion.
May each stitch be a seed of joy.
May each stitch be a seed of grace.
May each stitch be a seed of love.

—WREN ROSS
BOSTON, MASSACHUSETTS

T

HIS PATTERN IS BASED ON A CHRISTENING

baby wrap knitted by Sheila McNeil and submitted by

Helen MacLennon of Our Lady of Perpetual Help in Halifax. Adapted for a prayer

shawl by Vicky Cole-Galo, this intermediate pattern is based on multiples of 14 +10.

The Merino wool yarn used for this shawl was donated by Melissa Hickey in honor of her mother,

Maria Mendes, who was an avid knitter.

FROM
Sheila McNeil
Halifax, Nova Scotia,
Canada

FOREST PATH

Skill Level
Intermediate

Finished Measurements
54 in long and 25 in wide

Yarn
• Approximately 850 yd of worsted
 weight yarn
• Shawl shown in Lane Borgosesia Maratona
 (100% extra-fine Merino wool; 121 yd/
 1.75 oz), 7 skeins #8333 Dark Green

Needles
• Size 11 straight or circular needles
 (or size needed to obtain gauge)

Gauge
• 14 sts and 21 rows = 4 in worked
 in pattern

DIRECTIONS
CO on 94 sts. Knit 5 rows, then begin
pattern as follows:

Row 1: K5, *p2, k12, repeat from *
across, end k5.

Row 2: K5, *p10, k4, repeat from *
across, end k5.

Row 3: K5, *p6, p8, repeat from *
across, end k5.

Row 4: K5, *p6, p8, repeat from *
across, end k5.

Row 5: K5, *p10, k4, repeat from *
across, end k5.

Row 6: K5, *p2, k12, repeat from *
across, end k5.

Repeat Rows 1–6 to desired length,
ending with Row 6.

Knit 5 rows and BO all sts.

Shawl Maker's Journey

Many years ago, I received a beautiful shawl from Vicky Cole-Galo. The moment I saw the color of the shawl, felt its softness, and wrapped it around me, a shroud of spiritual power and love enveloped me.

Three years later, I was diagnosed with cancer. My shawl traveled with me as I walked a difficult path of treatment. I met many wonderful patients and caring professionals. One of these extraordinary professionals was my nurse, Mary. One day, while hooked up with IVs, I noticed Mary was not her usual bubbly self.

She told me that her mother passed away and that she and her sisters, Gerry and Janice, had grieved together. I knew I had to make a shawl for her. As I knit, I decided to make shawls for her sisters, too.

I was often tired during my recovery, but I had plenty of time to knit, so, before long, the three shawls were complete. At my next visit with Mary, I handed her the package. She held her shawl and said, "How thankful am I for our friendship." After a warm hug, she noticed the other shawls in the bag.

"Mary," I said, "I felt great love for you and your sisters, and I wanted the shawls to express my caring for them, also." The next time I saw Mary, she presented me with a beautiful knitting bag, a gift from them all. The shawls, she said, had created a unity they had not felt in years. "It was the prayerful instrument that bonded us again as sisters, loving and caring for one another and reassuring us that life would be okay."

JOSETTE STARKEY, Franklin, Tennessee

WHEN YOU WALKED AMONG US

Lord, when you walked among us, You embraced many. You embraced the young and the old. Your love gave life and courage to those who sought You. We, as Your disciples, carry on the work You began 2,000 years ago. The shawls we make are created with Your prayers upon our lips and Your prayers within our hearts. We pray that Your spirit of love, joy, and compassion be entwined in each thread. We pray that Your spirit of love and hope embrace those who receive our shawls. We pray that we may always be faithful servants of our loving Lord.

— MIKE KILEY
TINLEY PARK, ILLINOIS

DAKOTA WHEAT
SHAWL AND PIN

THIS LOVELY DIAGONALLY STRIPED SHAWL IS KNIT entirely in Garter Stitch, using three wonderfully soft mohair-blend yarns. The ladies who make Decadent Fibers yarn, in which the shawl shown here is knit, hand-dye their beautiful yarns—these shades of gold, brown, and green reminded designer Kathleen Taylor of a South Dakota wheat field. You can make the shawl pin easily with a little wire and some glass beads.

Skill Level
Easy

Finished Measurements
99 in long and 18 in wide, blocked

Yarn
- Approx 490 yd worsted weight brushed mohair (Color A)
- Approx 490 yd worsted weight looped mohair (Color B)
- Approx 490 yd worsted weight looped mohair (Color C)
- Shawl shown in Decadent Fibers Cotton Candy brushed mohair (78% mohair/13% wool/9% nylon; 490 yd/8 oz), 1 skein Variegated Golds; Decadent Fibers Life Saver loop mohair (78% mohair/13% wool/9% nylon; 490 yd/8 oz), 1 skein each Variegated Golds and Variegated Golds/Greens/Browns

Needles
- Size 13 straight needles, 10 in long (or size needed to obtain gauge)
- Crochet hook

Notions for Shawl
- Safety pin (optional)

Gauge
- 8½ sts and 16 rows = 4 in worked in Garter Stitch

KATHLEEN TAYLOR'S
DAKOTA WHEAT

Shawl

DIRECTIONS

Note: It may help to mark RS of shawl with a safety pin.
With Color A, CO 40 sts.

Row 1 (WS): Knit across. Turn.

Row 2 (RS): K1, inc 1, knit to last 2 sts, k2tog. Turn.

Rows 3–16: Repeat Rows 1–2. Change to Color B and repeat Rows 1–16.

Change to Color C and repeat Rows 1–16.

Repeat the entire color sequence 5 times, ending with an additional 16-row section of Color A. BO.

FINISHING

Weave in loose ends. Wash and block shawl to listed measurements.

Note: Hand-dyed yarns, such as the ones used for this shawl, can bleed. Before pinning a wet shawl to any surface (such as a rug or bed) test colorfastness of yarn and surface you will pin it to.

FRINGE

After shawl is blocked and dry, cut 80 18-in lengths of each of the 3 yarns. Hold 1 strand of each yarn tog and fold strands in half, then attach fringe (see pp. 167–168) in each st along the CO and BO edges of shawl.

Notions for Pin

- 1 wooden chopstick, cut to 6 in long
- Sandpaper
- Black paint, if needed
- Wire cutters
- 20-gauge silver-coated wire, 24 in
- Needle-nose jewelry pliers
- Mainstay Crafts Glass E Beads, 1 tube 80244-03 Opal Lined
- Glass Elements Beads: 1 package each of 35 g Amber Assortment, Medium; 10 mm by 13 mm Glass Swirl Beads #740 Topaz

Pin

DIRECTIONS

Step 1: Sand the cut chopstick and paint it black, if necessary. (**Note:** You can use a black permanent marker instead of paint, if desired.)

Step 2: Cut wire to size. Using pliers, bend a small loop in one end of wire (Figure 1). Place beads on wire in this sequence: 1 light E bead, 1 dark E bead, 1 Topaz Swirl Bead, 1 dark E bead, 1 light E bead, 1 Amber Assortment bead, 1 light E bead, 1 dark E Bead, 1 Amber Assortment bead. Repeat until the wire is full, with ½ in empty on either end. Use pliers to bend a small loop in other end of wire.

Step 3: Following Figure 2, bend wire in half, and lightly twist strands around each other.

Step 4: Bend twisted wire into a circle about 4 in in diameter. Twist ends of wire tog, and then twist those wires around the circle to hide ends.

Figure 1. Pin Beading

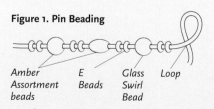

Amber Assortment beads   E Beads   Glass Swirl Bead   Loop

Figure 2. Beaded Wire

Fold in center, twist beaded strands around each other. Leave ½ in unbeaded at each end of wire.

Socks and Shawls

I knit mostly for the pleasure that knitting gives me, and for the pleasure that those knitted things bring to others. And the majority of my giveaways are socks. In fact, if I had been invited to submit a design and story to a Prayer *Sock* Ministry book, I would have had my project finished well before the deadline. As it turned out, designing my shawl proved a challenge.

I knew immediately who would get this shawl. My good friend Shirley was grappling with the end stages of her husband's terminal cancer. She and Dick met this adventure head-on, with the kind of humor, grace, and courage that I can only hope to achieve.

I knew immediately what yarns I wanted to use. I'd been sent a box of hand-dyed yarns from Decadent Fibers in Kinderhook, New York. The mohair I chose looked like a South Dakota wheat field—browns for the bare soil, greens for the emerging crop, and glorious golds for the harvest. Shirley and Dick were both from South Dakota; I wanted to knit something special to keep Shirley warm, and to give her a hug when she needed one.

I originally thought that knitting a shawl would be quick and easy: big needles, thick yarn when I'm used to fingering weight, simple garter stitch. But it wasn't.

I worked out a three-panel design, with increases on every right-side row, but I kept losing track of which was the right side. I wasn't happy with the shawl, and the yarn wasn't happy with what I was forcing it to do. After struggling for about 10 days, I tore it out. I worked out a triangle design and gave it a go, but the yarn didn't look good in that pattern, either.

Dejected, I sat and looked at that beautiful yarn, wishing that I was knitting socks for Shirley instead.

I looked at the yarn again, and this time, I listened to it. Beginning again, I worked out a simple repeat with the greens and browns nestled between swaths of gold, and an even simpler pattern that resulted in diagonal stripes along the shawl. Finally, the yarn was satisfied, and Shirley's Dakota Wheat Shawl grew and grew. Long enough to keep Shirley warm on chilly evenings. Long enough to wrap around her twice. Long enough to surround her with the love I knit into every stitch—for her, and for Dick, who passed away before the shawl was finished. Long enough to hold her through the next harvest.

KATHLEEN TAYLOR,
Northeastern South Dakota

T HESE TWO SHAWLS ARE SMALLER VERSIONS OF THE ORIGINAL
prayer shawl pattern, based on the knit three, purl three pattern. They can be used
as baby gifts or knitted for baptisms, christenings, or baby naming ceremonies. They
may also be given to any child as a source of comfort and solace. The first pattern is
by Janet Bristow and the second is from Susan Meader Tobias.

BAPTISM SHAWLS

FROM
Janet Bristow
Farmington, Connecticut

Rectangle Baptism Shawl

Skill Level
Easy

Finished Measurements
31 in long and 13 in wide (without edging)

Yarn
- Approx 350 yd worsted weight yarn
- Shawl shown in Caron Perfect Match® (100% acrylic; 355 yd/7 oz), 1 skein #7401 Baby Rainbow Ombre

Needles
- Size 10 straight or circular needles (or size needed to obtain gauge)
- Size G crochet hook (optional)

Gauge
- 15 sts and 25 rows = 4 in worked in k3, p3 pattern

DIRECTIONS
CO 21 or 24 sts, or number for desired width (number of sts must be a multiple of 3).

Row 1: K3, p3 across.

Row 2: Knit the purl sts and purl the knit sts as they face you.

Work as established until shawl is 31 in or desired length. BO all sts.

FINISHING
Add fringe (see pp. 167–168) or crochet a simple ch-st edging, as follows: Attach yarn in one corner of shawl with a sc, *ch 5, sk 1 st, work 1 sc in next st, repeat from * around shawl.

FROM
Susan Meader
Tobias
Washington, D.C.

Triangle Baptism Shawl

Skill Level
Easy

Finished Measurements
45 in long and 20 in deep

Yarn
- Approx 180 yd worsted weight yarn
- Shawl shown in Bernat Baby Bouclé (97% acrylic/3% polyester; 180 yd/ 3.5 oz), 1 skein #00104 Soft Lemon

Needles
- Size 13 straight or circular needle (or size needed to obtain gauge)

Notions
- Stitch markers

Gauge
- 12 sts and 14 rows = 4 in worked in 3-St Pattern

DIRECTIONS
CO 3 sts.

Row 1: Inc 1 st in each st. (6 sts)

Row 2: K3, p3 across.

Rows 3–99: Inc 1 st at beginning of every row, maintaining the 3-St Pattern by purling the knits and knitting the purls as they face you. You may need to use markers to help keep track of the 3-st repeats, because each row will be different.

BO loosely.

Pink Shawls for Two

One day I received a call from the pastor of our congregation asking if I could quickly make a baby shawl. Prayers were needed for a newborn who had been born prematurely.

I think God had known this request would be coming. Some time before this, I had started a pink shawl. I knew I had only enough yarn to knit about half of the usual 6-ft length of a prayer shawl, but I didn't worry about that because this was "no-dye-lot" yarn, and I could go back and get another matching skein at any time. No such luck. I carried a piece of the yarn with me for months, checking every store I went into, but the new yarns were all a bit darker. So my half-done shawl lay in my knitting basket until that phone call telling me of the new baby who had come so early. I picked up the pink in-process shawl, ripped out a few rows to get enough yarn for the fringe, and was able to finish the baby-size shawl in just one day.

Shortly after this, another tiny baby girl was born. This time, I knitted another little pink prayer shawl from scratch. And now, almost 2 years later, these two tiny babies have grown to be beautiful, energetic little girls who run around our church halls. The blessings in these shawls have returned to us many-fold.

Seeing a shawl being blessed is very rewarding; I feel its warmth as if it were around my shoulders. Being a part of this ministry that is not so quiet anymore and seeing it grow from person to person is very special to me.

BARBARA FOX, Eagan, Minnesota

BLESSING FOR MOTHER AND CHILD

Loving God,
Bless this woman and the new life she has birthed into the world.
As she swaddles her baby, may she too be enfolded in Your unconditional, motherly embrace.
Precious these two lives, forever bonded to each other—and to You!
Amen

—JANET BRISTOW

This shawl is just right for a mother to wrap herself and her child in while nursing, providing a private space for nursing or just cuddling. Consider making this shawl a bit longer so that it can easily drape around mother and baby. Note that fringe might not be a good idea for this shawl, but a nice crocheted border enhanced by a coordinating ribbon, adds just the right touch. And, of course, please select a yarn that can be machine washed and dried.

FROM
Janet Bristow

NURSING SHAWL

Skill Level
Easy

Finished Measurements
55 in long and 23 in wide

Yarn
- Approx 555 yd worsted weight bouclé yarn
- Shawl shown in Bernat Baby Bouclé
  (97% acrylic/3% polyester; 180 yd/3.5 oz),
  4 skeins #36922 Fancy Free

Trim
- 2 yd ¼-in satin ribbon

Needles
- Size 11 straight or circular needles
  (or size needed to obtain gauge)
- Size J or K crochet hook

Gauge
- 9 sts and 17 rows = 4 in worked in pattern

DIRECTIONS
CO 57 sts.

Row 1: Work k3, p3 across.

Row 2: Work k3, p3 across, being sure to knit the purl stitches and purl the knit stitches as they face you.

Repeat Rows 1 and 2 until shawl reaches from fingertip to fingertip, or desired length. BO all sts.

FINISHING
With crochet hook, attach yarn on one end of shawl with a sc. Work edging as follows: *Sk 2 sts, work 5 dc in next st, sk 2 sts, sc in next st, repeat from * across. Repeat on other end. Weave satin ribbon through holes created by dc clusters and tie in a double knot at ends to secure.

PRAYER SHAWL FOR A NEW MOTHER

*Prayers and loving thoughts were woven into the stitches
of this prayer shawl as it was made for you.
May it be a sign of God's constant caring presence and His abiding love.
May it remind you to be ever thankful of your unique God-given gifts.
May it remind you of the answer to your prayers, this miracle of new life.
May it encircle you with warmth and comfort when you are tired and stressed.
May hosts of angels surround and protect you and your babies.
May God's generous blessings be bestowed on you and your babies as it warms you.
May God bless you as new parents and grant you strength and wisdom along the way.
In wonder and thanksgiving, may you enjoy watching your precious little children grow.
Enjoy the shawl made with love, hugs, and prayers, and remember to trust in the Lord.*

—CECILE GANNON
EDMONTON, ALBERTA, CANADA

Blessings from Above

Our son and daughter-in-law returned from Germany one year to spend Christmas the holidays and to make a surprise announcement: "We're pregnant!" With tear-filled eyes, we shared their joy. A month later, we learned they were expecting twins. Unfortunately, one baby appeared to be much smaller than the other, and the doctor warned them that it may not survive.

After hearing about the Prayer Shawl Ministry, I hurried to make a prayer shawl for the mother. I worked for hours, praying for a safe delivery and two healthy babies. When my husband was around, he joined in the prayers.

When our son and his wife returned to Canada, I was just finishing the shawl. Our parish priest blessed it, and we drove over to their house to present it to them. Together, we stood around my daughter-in-law while I wrapped it over her shoulders and said a little prayer I had composed. Later, after a medical checkup, they were told the pregnancy seemed to be coming along fine, and my son returned overseas to complete some unfinished work.

No sooner had he landed when our daughter-in-law had to be admitted to the hospital. Packing quickly, she tucked the prayer shawl along with her belongings. That same evening, an emergency caesarian section was performed. At two and a half months before her due date, with her husband away, she called our daughter—a medical doctor—to accompany her in the operating room.

She asked the doctors if she could bring the prayer shawl into the operating room. Regretfully, they refused because it was not sterile. Our daughter told her, "Don't worry, I'll snip the small shell attached to the fringe, and together we will hold it in our hand during the surgery. Later, we can reattach it." They held the small, sterile relic during the delivery, and on May 25, 2006, two fragile babies entered the world, a 2-pound girl and a 3-pound boy. They were whisked off to the neonatal intensive care unit (where they remained for 55 days). Our drowsy daughter-in-law lay resting in bed with the prayer shawl spread over her.

The shawl was wrapped around her shoulders the next day as we wheeled her to visit the babies for the first time. After that, she draped the prayer shawl over the incubator of whichever baby seemed to be struggling. When the twins arrived home, I presented each one with a prayer shawl, too. Today, the babies are healthy, smiling, and thriving on tender loving care. They are the pride and joy of their parents, who thank God daily for their generous blessing.

CECILE GANNON
Edmonton, Alberta, Canada

FROM
Susan Berberich
Brunswick, Maine

OUR WORKSHOPS HAVE GIVEN US AN OPPOR-tunity to meet face to face with many prayer shawl makers, such as Susan Berberich, who designed this shawl. This amazing and graceful woman has added so much to our ministry, from being a valued member of the online message board community to being a founding member of the Sew Blessed Ministry of Saint John the Baptist Church in Brunswick, Maine. The inspiration for this child's shawl comes from Susan's young granddaughters, Zoe Cate and Carmin Marie, who informed Susan one day that a prayer is a hug you give a person when she's away from you. As Susan remarks, prayer is "God's way of hugging us all. And isn't that what we all do with the shawls—pray hugs into them?"

HUGS FROM MY ANGEL

Skill Level
Intermediate

Finished Measurements
33 in long and 17 in deep

Yarn
- Approx 250 yd worsted weight yarn
- Shawl shown in Caron Wintuk® (100% Acrilan® acrylic; 150 yd/3 oz), 2 skeins #3001 White

Needles
- Size 10 straight or circular needles (or size needed to obtain gauge)

Notions
- Stitch markers

Gauge
- 28 sts and 28 rows = 4 in worked in Trinity Pattern

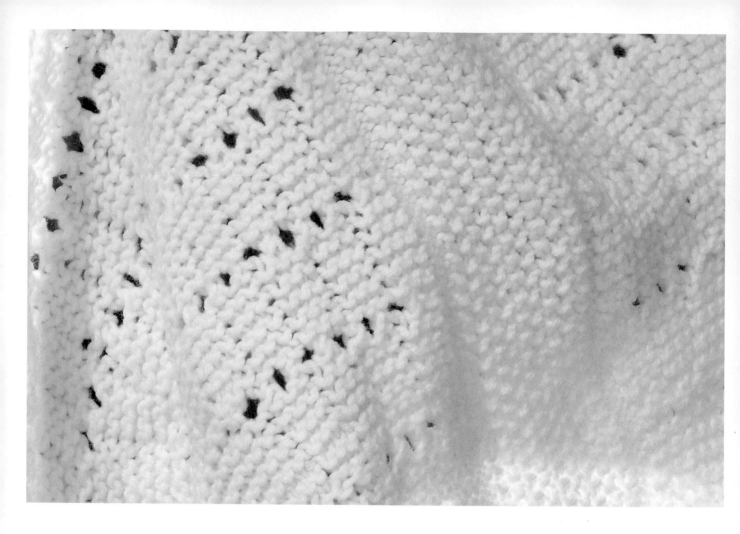

BORNE

Like a butterfly emerging from its cocoon, a shawl   skeins of yarn. Wings to fly above troubled water

is   from

~~~Envelopment   unfurled   Solace~~~

~~~~~~~~   ~~~~~~~

Shelter   Peace

~~~~~~~~   ~~~~~~~~~

Comfort   Rest

~~~~~~~~   ~~~~~~~~

Security   Sacred

~~~~~~~~   ~~~~~~~~

Warmth

—JANET BRISTOW

HUGS FROM MY ANGEL

DIRECTIONS

CO 111 sts.

Knit across the first row, placing markers after sts 4, 49, 51, 60, 62, and 107. These will be slipped as you go along and indicate where a pattern change occurs.

Row 1: Knit across to third marker. At st 52 (beginning of center section), work Seed Stitch over next 9 sts between markers as follows: (K1, p1) 4 times, end k1. After next marker (st 60), knit across to end, slipping markers from left needle to right.

Row 2: K4, sl marker, work Trinity Pattern as follows: (k3, p3) 7 times, end k3. Sl marker, p2, sl marker, work Seed Stitch across next 9 sts. Sl marker, p2, sl marker, work Trinity Pattern, sl marker, k4.

Row 3: K4, work Trinity Pattern to marker, k2, work Seed Stitch to marker, k2, work Trinity Pattern to marker, k4.

Row 4: K4, work Trinity Pattern to marker, p2, work Seed Stitch to marker, p2, work Trinity Pattern to marker, k4.

Rows 5, 7, 9, and 11: Repeat Row 3.

Row 6, 8, 10, and 12: Repeat Row 4.

Row 13 (Dec Row): Note: As you work, move markers as indicated.

K2tog 4 times (remove first marker when you approach it and replace it after fourth k2tog), k2tog 2 times. (dec 6 sts) (Yo, k2tog) across to 1 st before next marker, k1, sl marker, k2, sl marker, work Seed Stitch to marker, sl marker, k2, sl marker, k1, (k2tog, yo) across to last

12 sts. K2tog 6 times, removing last marker. (Each wing section now has 39 sts remaining.)

Row 14: K4, replace marker removed in last row, work Trinity Pattern to marker (**Note:** After knitting or purling each yo, give yarn a little tug when working next st to take up slack left from yo), p2, work Seed Stitch to marker, p2, work Trinity Pattern to marker, k4.

Rows 15, 17, 19, 21, and 23: Repeat Rows 3.

Rows 16, 18, 20, 22, and 24: Repeat Row 4.

Row 25 (Dec Row): Repeat Row 13. (Each wing section now has 33 sts remaining.)

Row 26: Repeat Row 14.

Rows 27, 29, 31, 33, and 35: Repeat Row 3.

Rows 28, 30, 32, 34, and 36: Repeat Row 4.

Row 37 (Dec Row): Repeat Row 13. (Each wing section now has 27 sts remaining.)

Row 38: Repeat Row 14.

Rows 39, 41, 43, 45, and 47: Repeat Row 3.

Rows 40, 42, 44, 46, and 48: Repeat Row 4.

Row 49 (Dec Row): Repeat Row 13. (Each wing section now has 21 sts remaining.)

Row 50: Repeat Row 14.

Rows 51, 53, 55, 57, and 59: Repeat Row 3.

Rows 52, 54, 56, 58, and 60: Repeat Row 4.

continued

HUGS FROM MY ANGEL

Row 61 (Dec Row): Repeat Row 13. (Each wing section now has 15 sts remaining.)

Row 62: Repeat Row 14.

Rows 63, 65, 67, 69, and 71: Repeat Row 3.

Rows 64, 66, 68, 70, and 72: Repeat Row 4.

Row 73 (Dec Row): K2tog 4 times (remove first marker when you approach it and replace it after fourth k2tog), k2tog 2 times, yo, k2tog, k1, sl marker, k2, sl marker, work Seed Stitch to marker, sl marker, k2, sl marker, k1, k2tog, yo, k2tog 6 times. (Each wing section now has 9 sts remaining.)

Row 74: Repeat Row 14.

Rows 75, 77, 79, 81, and 83: Repeat Row 3.

Rows 76, 78, 80, 82, and 84: Repeat Row 4

Row 85 (Dec Row): K2tog 4 times (remove first marker when you approach it and replace it after fourth k2tog), k2tog 2 times, k1, sl marker, k2, sl marker, work Seed Stitch to marker, sl marker, k2, sl marker, k1, k2tog 6 times. (Each wing section now has 3 sts remaining.)

Rows 86, 88, 90, 92, and 94: K4 (remove first marker when you approach it and replace it after fourth knit st), k3, sl marker, p2, sl marker, work Seed Stitch to marker, sl marker, p2, sl marker, k3, sl marker, k4.

Rows 87, 89, 91, 93, and 95: K4, sl marker, k3, sl marker, k2, sl marker, work Seed Stitch to marker, sl marker, k2, sl marker, k3, sl marker, k4.

Row 96: Continue in pattern, removing all markers as you work across.

Row 97 (Final Dec Row): K2tog 6 times, p1, k1, p1, k2tog 6 times.

Row 98: (**Note:** For this row, work Seed Stitch over the 7 remaining sts in center section.) K4, replace marker, (p1, k1) 3 times, end p1, replace marker, k4.

Rows 99–102: Repeat Row 98.

Row 103: K2tog 3 times, p1, k1, p1, k2tog 3 times.

Row 104: K3, p1, k1, p1, k3.

Row 105: K2tog 2 times, k1, k2tog 2 times.

Row 106: K5.

Row 107: K2tog, k1, k2tog.

Row 108: K3.

Row 109: K2tog, k1.

Row 110: K2tog. Pull yarn through last st to fasten off.

FINISHING

If desired, add a fringe. Cut 3 lengths of yarn 6 in long. Fold in half and pull through final stitch as shown on pp. 167–168.

Pink for Marilyn

I've been knitting prayer shawls for about 5 years and have started a group at my church. I always carry a work-in-progress every place I go just in case I have a few minutes to add another row—or more.

In February 2006, I went with a church group to New Orleans to help the Katrina victims. Of course, my shawl knitting went along. For some reason, I was using a bright pink yarn, not my usual choice, which is any shade of blue. On the long bus ride from Wisconsin to New Orleans, I knit and knit and knit some more.

In New Orleans, we were assigned to help several families, but I mostly helped a woman named Marilyn. She had had 10 ft of water in her house and had lost almost all of her material possessions. She had fled to Houston. The first time she had been back was when we were there with her, 5 months after the storm. She touched me with her stories—her own story; the stories of friends, neighbors, and relatives who did not survive; and the amazing stories of those who did, clinging to life on bridges and overpasses.

After 5 days of gutting her house and thoroughly bleaching the studs, floors, and ceilings, we exchanged addresses and phone numbers, and after hugs and tears, we said our good-byes. I got back on the bus and, after a long nap, picked up my knitting. *This one is for Marilyn,* I decided. *The color is perfect—happy, cheerful, and bight pink.* So that was the reason for the pink. I mailed it to her after I got home, and now she calls me her angel. She touched me. She showed me dignity and hope, how precious and fragile life is, and what it means to trust. I learned from Marilyn that we need to take care of each other. A touch, a hug, an arm around the shoulder are just as important as the big stuff.

MARY KIRCHHOFF
Mukwonago, Wisconsin

TALLIS

MELISSA MATTHAY HAS CREATED A KEEPSAKE *tallis*, or Jewish prayer shawl, which you can customize for your own young loved one's Bar or Bat Mitzvah. This pattern is deceptively easy to make—the beaded *atarah* (neckpiece) was purchased separately from a Judaic supply source (Melissa recommends www.ahuva.com) and sewn on after the shawl was knit. Traditional *tzitzit* (knotted fringe) may be added to each corner (instructions can be found online).

Skill Level
Easy

Finished Measurements
26 in wide and 64 in long

Yarn
- Approx 400 yd DK weight fur yarn (Color A)
- Approx 80 yd bulky metallic eyelash yarn (Color B)
- Approx 130 yd worsted weight metallic yarn (Color C)
- Approx 300 yd worsted weight ribbon yarn with metallic slubs (Color D)
- Approx 80 yd bulky metallic eyelash yarn (Color E)
- Shawl shown in Lion Brand Yarn Tiffany (100% nylon; 137 yd/1.75 oz), 3 skeins #260-100 White (Color A); Lana Gatto Crystal (63% viscose/20% nylon/17% polyester; 87 yd/1.75 oz), 1 skein #4117 Silver (Color B); Lion Brand Yarn Glitterspun (60% acrylic, 27% Cupro, 13% polyester; 115 yd/1.75 oz), 2 skeins #990-150 Silver (Color C); GGH Stars (86% polyamide/14% polyester; 143 yd/1.75 oz), 2 skeins #6 Twinkle (Color D); Lana Gatto Crystal (63% viscose/20% nylon/17% polyester; 87 yd/1.75 oz), 1 skein #4118 Bluc (Color E)

Needles
- Size 10½ straight needles (or size needed to obtain gauge)

Notions
- Purchased *atarah* (neckpiece)
- Pins (straight or safety)
- Sewing needle and thread to match *atarah*

Gauge
- 12 sts and 18 rows = 4 in worked in Stockinette Stitch

MELISSA MATTHAY'S
TALLIS

DIRECTIONS
With Color E, CO 59 sts. Working in Stockinette Stitch, follow the following Stripe Pattern:

STRIPE PATTERN

8 rows Color C	2 rows Color D	1 row Color D
2 rows Color E	2 rows Color A	3 rows Color A
2 rows Color C	1 row Color D	1 row Color D
4 rows Color A	3 rows Color A	2 rows Color A
2 rows Color E	1 row Color D	2 rows Color D
2 rows Color C	2 rows Color A	4 rows Color C
2 rows Color A	2 rows Color D	2 rows Color B
1 row Color C	4 rows Color C	6 rows Color A
3 rows Color A	4 rows Color B	2 rows Color E
1 row Color C	4 rows Color A,	6 rows Color A
3 rows Color A	8 rows Color B	2 rows Color C
2 rows Color C	4 rows Color A	4 rows Color A
2 rows Color E	4 rows Color B	2 rows Color C
4 rows Color A	4 rows Color C	3 rows Color A
4 rows Color B	2 rows Color D	1 row Color E
4 rows Color C	2 rows Color A	

You have now worked to the middle of shawl. Starting with 1 row Color E, work Stripe Pattern backward to end. **Note:** You will have 2 rows of Color E in middle of tallis.

With Color E, *BO first 5 sts, drop 6th st, leaving a space; repeat from *, BO last 5 sts.

Gently pull dropped sts so they unravel all the way to other end of shawl.

Weave in end. To each of the four corners, add *tzitzit*, if desired, or fringe (pp. 167–168), as shown in the photo.

ATTACHING THE *ATARAH*

Fold completed shawl in half, marking center of shawl at neckline with a pin. Find center back neck point of *atarah* and mark it with a pin. Place *atarah* over shawl so neckline edges match and center back neck points match. Baste *atarah* in place, then hand-stitch to shawl with sewing needle and matching thread.

WHAT YOU WOVE

I wear this raiment now
and think of the hours spent
in the making—
crossing, clicking sticks as the seconds
on a clock tick—
the interwoven wool locking
as fingers lock
around my heart, quieting
my breath,
holding my body still.

In the dark hour I sit,
wrapped against worry
in indigo string and violet blue
and charms crowned by
solid knots—
my grandmother's pearl, a silver star,
a circular winking cat.

I wear what you wove to
protect me—
the work of your craft, a healer,
a totem, a talisman between
a wheeling
world and this body that doubts
and unravels.

But there is surety in this fiber,
weight, strength, and heft
on my shoulders, like your hands
that wove in triplicate weave
hope with hope with hope.

—AMANDA BRISTOW
CAMBRIDGE, MASSACHUSETT

Sophie's *Tallis*

I knit this shawl at the request of my 13-year-old niece, Sophie, who also needed an outfit to wear for her Bat Mitzvah. The Bat Mitzvah is the ceremony in which girls are recognized as Jewish adults, and they receive the prayer shawl that they will use through adulthood. Traditionally, only men were allowed to receive and wear a *tallis*. But now, in the Reform and Reconstructionist Jewish movements—to which Sophie belongs—women may do so, too. These prayer shawls often are handed down through the generations.

"Aunt Lissy," she asked me, "would you knit me hot pink bell-bottom pants?" I laughed and said, "You'll never be able to sit down." I began sketching some other ideas on a napkin, and we ended up with a cute miniskirt with a ruffled bottom, and a jacket with bell sleeves. But this was just what she would wear while walking up to the altar to receive her *tallis*—her prayer shawl. The real honor, for me, was making that.

Knitting Sophie's *tallis* felt very spiritual, very soothing, very special—even magical. I kept thinking, "This is the prayer shawl she'll have the rest of her life. This is something that will become her heirloom, handed down, not only blessing Sophie but also her children and grandchildren." I kept feeling God's presence as I knit. When you are consciously aware of doing God's work, when your heart is totally open to receiving God, you are incredibly blessed. Creating a prayer shawl is being attuned to God.

When Sophie came for her first fitting, nothing had to be changed. I like to think it's "a God thing." During the ceremony, I had the honor of standing at the altar and presenting Sophie with her prayer shawl. It was so beautiful—I got teary-eyed, as did Sophie's mom, my best friend since childhood. "Yes, there is a God," I thought, "and he's *huge*."

MELISSA MATTHAY
Madison, Wisconsin

WEDDING CAPELET

THIS CAPELET IS MADE IN THREE PIECES THAT ARE worked from the bottom up. Subtle decreases at the sides shape the shoulders for a beautiful fit. The edging is one of designer Nicky Epstein's favorites because the ribbing within the scallop forms a fan. The purchased pearl-beaded fringe gives the piece special elegance. The body is an all-over dash pattern that creates an easy textural effect. Repeating the scallops on the neck pulls the piece together and completes the capelet.

Skill Level
Experienced

Finished Measurements
44 in wide at lower edge (41 in wide at bust) and 16 in long

Yarn
- Approx 800 yd DK weight yarn
- Shawl shown in Berroco Softwist (59% rayon/41% wool; 100 yd/ 1.75 oz), 8 skeins #9401 Ivory

Needles
- Size 6 straight needles (or size needed to obtain gauge)
- Cable needle

Notions for Shawl
- Stitch markers
- Beaded trim, 80 in
- 1-in-wide ribbon, 45 in

Gauge
- 24 sts and 32 rows = 4 in worked in Dash Pattern

NICKY EPSTEIN'S
WEDDING CAPELET

SCALLOP PATTERN

Notes: St count will change with each row but will return to original number on Row 9.

Work ssk as follows: sl next st knitwise, sl next st purlwise, sl left-hand needle through these 2 sts and k2tog through back loop.

Setup Rows: Knit 1 row, purl 1 row, knit 1 row.

Row 1 (RS): K1, *yo, k21; repeat from *, end last repeat k23.

Row 2 (WS): P2, *[p1, k3] 5 times, p2; repeat from *, end last repeat p3.

Row 3: K1, *k1, yo, k1, [p3, k1] 5 times, yo; repeat from *, end k2.

Row 4: P1, *p3, [k3, p1] 5 times, p1; repeat from *, end last repeat p4.

Row 5: K1, *[k1, yo] twice, [ssk, p2] 5 times, [k1, yo] twice; repeat from *, end k2.

Row 6: P2, *p4, [k2, p1] 5 times, p4; repeat from *, end last repeat p5.

Row 7: K1, *[k1, yo] 4 times, [ssk, p1] 5 times, [k1, yo] 4 times; repeat from *, end k2.

Row 8: P2, *p8, [k1, p1] 5 times, p8; repeat from *, end last repeat p9.

Row 9: K1, *k8, [ssk] 5 times, k8; repeat from *, end last repeat p10.

Row 10: P2, *p12, sl last 4 sts to cable needle, wrap yarn clockwise around sts on cable needle 3 times, sl sts from cable needle back to right-hand needle, p9; repeat from *, end last repeat p10.

DASH PATTERN

Row 1 (WS): Purl.

Rows 2 and 4 (RS): Knit.

Row 3 and All WS Rows: Purl.

Row 6: P6, *k4, p6; repeat from *.

Rows 8 and 10: Knit.

Row 12: P1, *k4, p6; repeat from * to last 5 sts, k4, p1.

BACK

CO 171 sts. Work Setup Rows of Scallop Pattern, then Rows 1–10 of Scallop Pattern.

Next Row (RS): Knit, dec 35 sts evenly across row. (136 sts)

Change to Dash Pattern and work until piece measures approx 4¾ in above last row of Scallop Pattern, ending with a WS row.

Continue in Dash Pattern; *at the same time,* decrease 1 st each side every 4 rows 10 times, then every other row 8 times, ending with a WS row. (100 sts)

Shape shoulders and neck as follows:

Next Row (RS): BO 2 sts at beginning of next 4 rows, then 3 sts at beginning of next 2 rows. (86 sts)

Place markers at each side of center 22 sts.

Next Row: BO 3 sts, work to marker, join second ball of yarn and BO center 22 sts, work to end of row.

Next Row: Bind off 3 sts, working each side separately, work to end.

Working both sides at same time, continue in Dash Pattern as established; *at the same time,* BO at each side edge every other row 3 sts twice, then 4 sts once; *at the same time,* BO at each neck edge every other row 3 sts twice, then 2 sts once. BO remaining 11 sts on each side for shoulders.

LEFT FRONT

CO 87 sts. Work Setup Rows of Scallop Pattern, then Rows 1–10 of Scallop Pattern.

Next Row: Knit, dec 21 sts evenly across row. (66 sts)

Change to Dash Pattern and work until piece measures approx 4¾ in above last row of Scallop Pattern, ending with a WS row.

Continue in Dash Pattern; *at the same time,* dec 1 st at beginning of next row, then every 4 rows 9 more times, then every other row 8 times, ending with a RS row. (48 sts)

Shape neck and shoulders as follows:

Next Row (WS): BO 11 sts at beginning of row, work to end.

Continue in Dash Pattern as established; *at the*

same time, BO at side edge every other row 2 sts twice, 3 sts twice, 4 sts once; *at the same time,* BO at neck edge 3 sts twice, 2 sts twice, 1 st twice. BO remaining 11 sts for shoulder.

RIGHT FRONT
Work as for Left Front, reversing shaping.

FINISHING
Sew side seams.

Front Band: With RS facing, pick up 66 sts evenly spaced along front opening edge. Purl 1 row, knit 1 row, purl 1 row, BO loosely. **Note:** Band will roll to RS. Work remaining opening edge in same manner.

Collar: CO 108 sts. Work Setup Rows of Scallop Pattern, then Rows 1–10 of Scallop Pattern. Knit 1 row, purl 1 row. BO all sts. Sew collar to neck edge, ending just inside front bands.

Trim: Sew pearl trim around entire outer edge of capelet. Sew a 22½-in length of ribbon to each inside front edge of capelet at neck.

Knitting for Natalie

As a designer and author, I rarely have time to knit for a loved one. But when my godchild, Natalie, asked me to supply the "something new" for her wedding, I couldn't refuse. She wanted a small cover-up for her shoulders.

As I worked, I thought about Natalie's happiness and her bright future, and I was filled with a feeling of peace and love. Natalie was thrilled with the capelet—almost as thrilled as I was to be a part of her wedding.

Knitting for a loved one is an expression of love, creates a feeling of accomplishment, and is highly therapeutic. When you knit this shawl, choose a color that suits the occasion. You may choose from a variety of beaded fringes that are available in craft and fabric stores if you don't opt for the pearl fringe here.

NICKY EPSTEIN
New York, New York

Widthwise-Knit Shawl

THIS SIMPLE PATTERN IS KNIT lengthwise on circular needles, although it is easily made up widthwise as well. You simply knit three rows and then purl three rows. This creates a lovely shawl with a ridge effect and a nice drape. Any yarn will do. The shawl knitted lengthwise is knit in a worsted weight ribbon yarn; the shawl knit widthwise (at left) is made of a hand-dyed silk and wool yarn combined with a strand of silk and mohair yarn. This shawl is also knit with a technique known as "condo knitting," in which two different-size needles are used on every other row. The result is an open, lacy look with no extra effort. Have fun experimenting—the greater the difference in needle size, the lacier the effect.

FROM
Kathy Andreoli
West Hartford, Connecticut

THREEFOLD BLESSING SHAWL

Widthwise-Knit Shawl

Skill Level
Easy

Finished Measurements
60 in long and 19 in wide

Yarn
- Approx 600 yd bulky yarn
- Shawl shown in Alchemy Yarns Synchronicity (50% Merino wool/ 50% silk; 110 yd/1.75 oz), 6 skeins #64C Hidden Place, and Alchemy Yarns Haiku (60% mohair/40% silk; 325 yd/0.875 oz), 2 skeins #67E Topaz, 1 strand of each held tog

Needles
- Sizes 10 and 15 straight or circular needles (or sizes needed to obtain desired effect, using condo knitting)

Gauge
- 12 sts and 15 rows = 4 in worked in pattern stitch

DIRECTIONS
With larger needle, CO 57 sts.

Alternating larger and smaller needle, knit 3 rows, purl 3 rows until shawl measures 60 in or desired length.

BO all sts.

Add macramé fringe (see p. 168), if desired.

THREEFOLD BLESSING SHAWL

Lengthwise-Knit Shawl

Skill Level
Easy

Finished Measurements
63 in long and 15½ in wide

Yarn
- Approx 600 yd bulky yarn
- Shawl shown in Bernat Miami (100% acrylic; 81 yd/1.75 oz), 6 skeins #34714 Orangina

Needles
- Size 11 circular needles, at least 29 in long (or size needed to obtain gauge)

Gauge
- 14 sts and 18 rows = 4 in worked in pattern stitch

DIRECTIONS
CO 150 sts.

Knit 3 rows, purl 3 rows until shawl measures 18 in wide, or desired width.

BO all sts.

Add macramé fringe (see p. 168), if desired.

Lengthwise-Knit Shawl

What Are the Words?

Cate Rooney, 6 years old, is the granddaughter of my husband's twin sister, and a very dear little girl to me. She also has minimal change disease, which is a kidney disease that occurs in children. It's a treatable condition in most cases, though its effects are anything but "minimal." The tests and treatments can have serious side effects, are painful, and take a long time. When I heard about Cate's diagnosis, I wanted to do something for her. So I began making her a prayer shawl.

I showed Cate the start of her prayer shawl, and she wanted to watch me work on it. I told her the words I say to concentrate on the pattern and the prayers: "Creator loves Cate; Savior loves Cate; Sanctifier loves Cate" (for one set of three stitches) and "God the Father loves Cate; Son loves Cate; Holy Spirit loves Cate." I'll also simply say, "Faith, Hope, Love" (another set of three) or "Peace, Joy, Trust." I was grateful that Cate liked this shawl so much she wanted to make one herself. Her mom had yarn, I had needles, and her grandma had time to show her how.

The very next day, I got an urgent call from Cate's grandma: "What are the *words*?" she asked. I was somewhat confused until I finally realized that, for Cate, a necessary part of making her prayer shawl was asking for or feeling the presence of God. Knitting a prayer shawl simply wasn't complete without the prayer.

I don't know how far Cate got in her knitting (she is only 6, after all), but I do know that she sleeps with the prayer shawl I made her—though in San Diego, California, she hardly needs it for warmth. And shortly after she received it, she made me a drawing copying that prayer shawl in Magic Markers—a very special thank-you.

ANNIE BABSON, Montrose, California

THREEFOLD BLESSINGS

*Give threefold blessings as you
Stitch, pray, and create.*

*Extend threefold blessings as you
Reach out, touch, and enfold,*

*Receive threefold blessings to
Fill, encourage, and inspire you
To do it all over again.*

—JANET BRISTOW

LAP ROBE

THIS PRAYER BLANKET IS MADE FROM TWO STRANDS OF yarn knit together. Designer Carri Hammett combined the warmth and softness of a chunky-weight alpaca yarn with a beautiful and soft variegated fur yarn. The result is a delightfully soft fabric that has the weight of a favorite down comforter. Because it's knit using large needles, the work progresses quickly, and the fabric is quite stretchy. The final touch is a knitted I-cord edge that dresses up the blanket and gives it a tailored finish.

Skill Level
Easy

Finished Measurements
42 in long and 33 in wide

Yarn
- Approx 465 yd smooth bulky yarn (Color A)
- Approx 465 yd medium weight fur yarn (Color B)
- Approx 80 yd smooth bulky yarn (Color C)
- Shawl shown in Misti Alpaca Chunky (100% baby alpaca; 108 yd/3.5oz), 5 skeins #701 Marina Mélange (Color A); Colinette Silky Chic (100% nylon; 232 yd/3.5 oz); 2 skeins #90 Venezia (Color B); Misti Alpaca Chunky, 1 skein #7238 Chartreuse Mélange (Color C)

Note: Main body of lap robe is knit using Colors A and B held tog. I-cord trim is knit using C alone.

Needles
- Size 13 circular needle, at least 24 in long (or size needed to obtain gauge)
- Two size 10½ double-pointed needles

Notions
- Tapestry needle

Gauge
- 10 sts and 13 rows = 4 in worked in Seed Stitch

Note: If you tend to CO or BO too tightly, use a larger needle—size 13 or even 15—just for casting on or binding off. Use smaller needle for all other rows.

PSALM 34

I will praise the Lord at all times;
his praise is always on my lips.
My whole being praises the Lord.
The poor will hear and be glad.
Glorify the Lord with me,
and let us praise his name together.

I asked the Lord for help, and he answered me.
He saved me from all that I feared.
Those who go to him for help are happy,
and they are never disgraced.
This poor man called, and the Lord heard him
and saved him from all his troubles.
The angel of the Lord camps around those who
fear God,
and he saves them. . . .

The Lord sees the good people
and listens to their prayers.
But the Lord is against those who do evil;
he makes the world forget them.
The Lord hears good people when they cry out
to him,
and he saves them from all their
troubles.
The Lord is close to the brokenhearted
and he saves those whose spirits have
been crushed.

People who do what is right may have many
problems,
but the Lord will solve them all.
He will protect their very bones;
not one of them will be broken. . . .

(NEW CENTURY VERSION)

CARRI HAMMETT'S
LAP ROBE

DIRECTIONS
With Colors A and B held tog, CO 75 sts.

Row 1: *K1, p1*, repeat from * to * until 1 st remains, end with k1.

Row 2: Repeat Row 1.
Repeat Rows 1 and 2 until lap robe measures approx 40 in, or desired length.

BO all sts loosely knitwise.

I-CORD BINDING
Work I-cord binding in Color C alone. The easiest way to work I-cord is by using 2 balls of yarn. Begin by winding approx one third of yarn into a smaller ball.

Using smaller ball and starting in middle of BO edge (not at a corner) begin by picking up and knitting about 4 in worth of sts onto one double-pointed needle. You should aim to pick up at a rate of about 3½ sts per in. Because blanket is knit using much larger sts, you will need to pick up about 4 sts from every 3 sts on blanket.

Once you've picked up the group of sts, go back to beginning (where yarn tail is). Using larger ball of yarn, CO 3 new sts using a knitted CO (see p. 167). (These new sts won't be attached to blanket.) Tighten up the two yarn tails (tie half of a square knot if desired).

Using larger ball of yarn and second double-pointed needle, start knitting I-cord as follows:

Row 1: K2, ssk, then transfer 3 sts from right needle back to left needle.

Repeat Row 1 until just a few sts (3 or 4 sts) remain on left needle. Using smaller ball of yarn, pick up a new group of sts as before. Switch back to larger ball of yarn and continue making I-cord as established.

Continue in this manner until entire blanket has been edged and you've used the last picked-up st. To finish, BO final 3 sts.

Hint: When you get to corners, pick up a few extra sts close tog so I-cord binding can form a miter around corner.

FINISHING

Using a tapestry needle and Color C, join ends of I-cord binding tog. Weave in all ends.

My Father's Lap Robe

Several years ago, I had to have very serious surgery, and I was more than a little apprehensive. I gave my husband a soft fleece blanket to keep while I was in surgery. I asked him to tuck the blanket around me after I was out of surgery and back in my hospital room. I knew that, even unconsciously, I would feel the softness and warmth of the blanket on my shoulders and face. For me, that would be a signal that I had made it through the surgery and I was on the road to recovery. More important, I would know that my husband was at my side.

A few years later, my father started to slip away to Alzheimer's disease and was confined to a wheelchair. I noticed that his sense of touch became very important to him. Although he could no longer hold a conversation, he would linger while holding someone's hand or stroking a soft blanket. I designed and knit a lap robe for him that would be very, very soft and warm. It was a "blankie" of sorts, but that's what my father needed in the dimming of his days. I made it in a size that could be laid across his lap as he sat in his chair or tucked up around his chin while he was sleeping. I could no longer talk to my dad with words, but I pray he was comforted by his blanket in the same way that I was touched by that simple fleece blanket in the hospital.

CARRI HAMMETT, Excelsior, Minnesota

STRIPED STOLE

BRANDON MABLY'S COLORFUL STOLE EXEMPLIFIES THE idea of a "gypsy shawl" and shows just what can be made of serendipity and the smallest of scraps. Worked on bit by bit, as the yarn came to Brandon, it eventually grew into a beautiful multicolored piece, finished elegantly with a taffeta lining. While his stole is worked in very fine, fingering weight yarns and small needles, you may wish to experiment with scraps of thicker yarns and fewer stitches for a quicker—but no less glorious—knit.

Skill Level
Easy

Finished Measurements
Approx 27 in by 84 in with edging

Yarn
- Approx 2,500 yd total of various fingering weight yarns and colors
- Shawl shown in various 4-ply Rowan Yarns

Needles
- Size 3 straight or circular needles (or size to obtain gauge)
- Size D crochet hook

Notions
- Approx 2½ yd taffeta (or other solid-color woven fabric) for lining (at least 36 in wide)
- Pins (straight or safety)
- Sewing needle and thread to match fabric for lining

Gauge
- 28 sts and 40 rows = 4 in worked in Stockinette Stitch

STRIPED STOLE

DIRECTIONS

CO 180 sts with desired color. Work in Stockinette Stitch (knit 1 row, purl 1 row), working first and last st in Garter Stitch (knit every row) for selvedge, using colors and yarns as desired for 83 in or desired length. BO.

EDGING

With RS facing, crochet hook, and desired color, work evenly around entire outside edge as follows:

Rnd 1: *Sc, ch 1, sk 1 st (or row); repeat from * evenly around outside edge, working (sc, ch 1, sc, ch 1) in each corner.

Rnds 2–4: With desired color, work sc, ch 1 in each ch-1 sp. Fasten off.

FINISHING

Weave in ends. Block to measurements.

Lay stole over lining fabric and cut lining same size as stole plus ½ in on all sides for seam allowance. Fold seam allowance under, press in place, and pin lining to inside of stole (with WS tog). With sewing needle and thread, hand-stitch lining in place.

Random Acts of Color

Several years ago, while teaching color workshops, I started collecting leftover bits of yarn. During classes and in my downtime, I began knitting them together, and what evolved is this glorious wrap. Colors were chosen randomly, then if sections became too dark, a kicker color was added; if too acidic, a somber hue was introduced to tone it down. Rounds of crochet were added to keep the edges from curling.

There is nothing more uplifting than sitting down and knitting on a project that incorporates deliciously exciting and unexpected color combinations. For me, it is like a meditation—running the yarns over my fingers, rubbing two needles together, forming a gorgeous web of colors that I hope will inspire others to have a go themselves.

When I'm designing, nothing goes on paper beforehand. The idea is conceived in my head, then on the needles by sitting and knitting a swatch before I write anything down. There is nothing more rewarding than working with color and inspiring others to step out of their box, have a go, and surprise themselves. I feel blessed to share my ideas and encourage others, too.

BRANDON MABLY
London, England

WORDS TO KNIT BY

'Tis a gift to be simple, 'tis a gift to be free,
'Tis a gift to come down where we ought to be,
...
To turn, turn will be our delight
'Till by turning, turning we come round right.

—OLD SHAKER HYMN

FROM
Jami Scott
Waldo, Wisconsin

THIS IS A BASIC PATTERN, SUITABLE FOR THE beginning knitter, which was developed for the launch of the Prayer Shawl Circle at First Congregational UCC in Plymouth, Wisconsin. The shawl is lozenge shaped (a rectangle with a triangular point on each end) and done in Stockinette Stitch with a Garter-Stitch border and a Reverse-Stockinette heart worked into one end. Instructions for a triangle-shaped version are also given.

WRAPPED IN LOVE

Skill Level
Beginner

Finished Measurements
68 in long and 39 in wide

Yarn
Note: For triangular version, divide yarn amounts in half.
- Approx 500 yd worsted weight cotton yarn
- Approx 500 yd worsted weight mohair or mohair-blend yarn
- Approx 500 yd smooth sport weight yarn
- Shawl shown in Elmore-Pisgah Peaches & Crème (100% cotton; 840 yd/16 oz), 1 cone #41 Light Grape; Red Heart Symphony™ (100% acrylic; 310 yd/3.5 oz), 2 skeins #4903 Mystic Purple; Bernat Softee Baby (100% acrylic; 455 yd/5 oz), 1 skein #30185 Soft Lilac

Needles
- Size 15 circular needle, 24 in long (or size needed to obtain gauge)
- Size M or N crochet hook

Notions
- Tapestry needle

Gauge
- 9 sts and 12 rows = 4 in worked in pattern, holding one strand of each yarn tog
Note: Hold one strand of each yarn tog, so three yarns are worked as one.

INCREASE SECTION

With all 3 yarns held tog, CO 4 sts.

Row 1: Knit across.

Row 2: K2, m1, knit across.

Row 3: K2, m1, purl across to last 2 sts, k2.

Repeat Rows 2 and 3 until you have 18 sts.

Row 14: K2, m1, k6, p1, knit across.

Row 15: K2, m1, p7, k1, purl across to last 2 sts, k2.

Row 16: K2, m1, k6, p3, knit across.

Row 17: K2, m1, p7, k3, purl across to last 2 sts, k2.

Row 18: K2, m1, k6, p5, knit across.

Row 19: K2, m1, p7, k5, purl across to last 2 sts, k2.

Row 20: K2, m1, k6, p7, knit across.

Row 21: K2, m1, p7, k7, purl across to last 2 sts, k2.

Row 22: K2, m1, k6, p9, knit across.

Row 23: K2, m1, p7, k9, purl across to last 2 sts, k2.

Row 24: K2, m1, k6, p11, knit across.

Row 25: K2, m1, p7, k11, purl across to last 2 sts, k2.

Row 26: K2, m1, k6, p13, knit across.

Row 27: K2, m1, p7, k13, purl across to last 2 sts, k2.

Row 28: K2, m1, k6, p15, knit across.

Row 29: K2, m1, p7, k15, purl across to last 2 sts, k2.

Row 30: K2, m1, k8, p15, knit across.

Row 31: K2, m1, p10, k6, p1, k6, purl across to last 2 sts, k2.

Row 32: K2, m1, k12, p4, k3, p4, knit across.

Row 33: K2, m1, p14, k2, p5, k2, purl across to last 2 sts, k2.

Row 34: Repeat Row 2.

Row 35: Repeat Row 3.

Repeat Rows 2 and 3 until piece is 24 in wide, or desired width, ending with Row 3.

CENTER SECTION

Row 1: K2, m1, k2tog, knit across.

Row 2: K2, m1, p2tog, purl across to last 2 sts, k2.

Repeat these rows until center section is 18 in long or desired length.

DECREASE SECTION

Row 1: K1, k2tog, m1, k2tog, knit across.

Row 2: K1, k2tog, m1, p2tog, purl across to last 2 sts, k2.

Repeat these rows until there are 4 sts remaining. BO.

FINISHING

Weave in ends. Add pompoms (see p. 168) or tassels (see p. 168) at beginning and ending points, if desired.

Triangle Shawl Option

DIRECTIONS

Follow Increase Section through Row 35.

Repeat Rows 2 and 3 until piece is desired width for long edge (neck edge) of triangular shawl. BO.

FINISHING

Weave in ends. If desired, add one or more of the following embellishments: (1) Work sc, with all 3 yarns held tog, along long edge for extra stability. (2) Add a pompom (see p. 168) or tassel (see p. 168) at beginning point. (3) Add I-cord (see p. 166) or crochet ties about one third of way up each end of long edge, so shawl may be tied tog.

Prayer Shawl for Mom and Honey

In September 2006, my mother-in-law was hospitalized. I prayed and knitted her a shawl while she slept. Later in the evening, she was alert and talking and holding her prayer shawl. Sadly, though, she did not make it through the night.

Later, when I was admitted to the hospital myself, I brought that shawl with me. My roommate was in the final stages of Alzheimer's disease. She became quite agitated and could no longer speak clearly. I thought maybe my shawl would help "Honey." This was a hard decision to make, because it was such a special shawl to me. But I thought, "Well, this is what the Prayer Shawl Ministry is all about," so when the nurse, whom I'll call Michelle, came in, we put the shawl on Honey.

Afterward, Honey was still chattering away, so I started to sing "Jesus Loves Me." She started to sing along with me, and though I had to listen closely to know she was singing, I definitely heard her say "Jesus" and "loves." What a blessing. I know she felt the love and comfort of God around her.

Later, I learned that Michelle had lost her grandson. Christmas Eve would have been his first birthday. She was really struggling with his loss. I knew I had to make Michelle a prayer shawl. When it was finished, I left it for Michelle at the hospital. I received the very nicest thank-you from her, in which she said she was beginning to have closure. God used prayer shawls to bless Mom, Honey, Michelle, and especially me.

ROBERTA LIGHTNER,
Duncannon, Pennsylvania

PRAYER OF WEAVING*

As many ancient women and men have woven before us and continue the weaving today, we ask God's blessings on our yarns, on our needles and crochet hooks.

God bless our hands and enlighten our minds as we weave our prayer shawls with love, for those known and unknown. We thank you, God, for the gift of weaving as we reach out to Your world in love.

Amen

—GLADYS P. COLE
NOKOMIS, FLORIDA

*This is the opening prayer used by the Prayer Shawl Ministry circle at Epiphany Catholic Cathedral, Venice, Florida.

THIS SHAWL IS A WONDERFUL WAY TO USE up odds and ends of yarns left over from shawls or other projects. You can choose a color and use yarns only in shades of that color, or make up your own colorway (based on autumn or ocean colors, for example), or make a "crazy shawl" of sorts, using any colors you happen to have. For more fun, share yarns from the stashes of your friends or those in your prayer shawl group.

FROM
Janet Bristow

TRAVELING SHAWL

Skill Level
Easy

Finished Measurements
76 (84) in long and 17 in wide

Yarn
- Approx 750 yd total of a variety of worsted to bulky weight yarns: smooth, chenille, eyelash, ribbon, thick-and-thin, and so on (thinner yarns may be combined to achieve desired weight)
- Shawl shown in a variety of yarns

Needles
- Size 13 circular needle, at least 29 in long (or size needed to obtain gauge)

Gauge
- 10 sts and 20 rows = 4 in worked in pattern

DIRECTIONS
Before casting on, allow for a long-enough tail of yarn for a fringe (12 in or desired length). With yarn of choice, CO 130 (150).

Row 1: K3, p3 across. At end of row, fasten off yarn and cut, leaving a tail of yarn same length as that on opposite end.

Row 2: Attach a new yarn, leaving enough for a fringe. Knit the purl sts and purl the knit sts as they face you. At end of row, fasten off yarn and cut, leaving a tail of yarn same length as established fringe.

Work as established, attaching new yarn for each row and leaving a tail for fringe on both ends, until shawl is desired width. BO all sts.

Sisterhood of the Shawl

Inspired by the movie *The Sisterhood of the Traveling Pants,* my girlfriends and I wondered what article of clothing we could all share. Because we were of all shapes and sizes, pants were out of the question. One friend said that a prayer shawl would fit everyone. She was right.

Unbeknownst to anyone else at that time, one woman in our group was facing major surgery at the end of summer. When I found this out, I thought it would be a great idea if we all made a "traveling prayer shawl." We prayed for each other as we knit, especially for the first recipient of the shawl, for whom it was a surprise. We kept a journal while we were knitting to see where the shawl traveled that summer and to read everyone's thoughts and prayers as they knit it. We decided that, in the true spirit of a traveling shawl, this one would be shared by everyone in the group during her own time of need.

At the end of the summer, we gathered at the home of the friend who was scheduled for surgery and prayed with her. She was asked to find a ribbon to lace through the stitches of the shawl as her contribution to it and to write her feelings and prayers in the journal as well. Since then, two other women in the group have had a need for the shawl. And both have found it very comforting and empowering.

RUTH SPRONG, Manchester, Connecticut

FINISHING
After body of shawl is complete, go back and fill in any spaces in the fringe. Knot together in groups of 4 to 6 strands, if desired, or weave in ends and attach tassels to corners (see p. 168).

KNIT 3, PURL 3 PRAYER

Know God, know Christ, know the Spirit.
Praise God, praise Christ, praise the Spirit.

— CATHERINE FOSTER
NORTHBORO, MASSACHUSETTS

THIS PATTERN WAS SENT TO US BY ANN CRIMMINS, of St. Petersburg, Florida, who knits prayer shawls with a group of women in her condominium. One of them is Fay Clarke, who provided this twist on the original knit three, purl three prayer shawl pattern. Fay began a shawl, but became frustrated when she discovered she had "messed up big time." She handed Ann her prayer shawl for examination. Upon study, Ann found that she was twisting stitches on one of the stripes. She didn't actually mess up; she created a whole new look. Her resulting shawl is delightful—comfortably close to the original pattern, but different enough to make a whole new creation.

FROM
Ann Crimmins
St. Petersburg, Florida

FAY'S WAY SHAWL

Skill Level
Easy

Finished Measurements
49 in long and 21 in wide

Yarn
- Approx 800 yd worsted weight yarn
- Shawl shown in Caron One Pound (100% acrylic; 812 yd/16 oz), 1 skein #535 Country Rose

Needles
- Size 11 straight or circular needles (or size needed to obtain gauge)

Gauge
- 12 sts and 18 rows = 4 in worked in Twisted Knit Stitch

DIRECTIONS
CO 63 sts.

Row 1: *K3, knitting into the back loop of each st (Twisted Knit Stitch), p3. Repeat from * to end of row, ending with 3 Twisted Knit Stitches.

Row 2: *Work 3 Twisted Knit Stitches, p3. Repeat from * to end of row, ending with 3 Twisted Knit Stitches.

Repeat Rows 1 and 2 until shawl measures 49 in, or desired length. BO all sts.

MY PRAYER

Creator God, who leads me to create, take the blessings I have in my hands into this yarn, through these needles, and into this prayer shawl. May these blessings be multiplied by the number of stitches until the receiver can feel Your love and the love from the people of this congregation.

—BARBARA FOX
EAGAN, MINNESOTA

God Will Provide

I had been praying that God would direct me in giving my first prayer shawl away until one day, when I was out with my family, and I struck up a conversation with a friendly stranger. She was wearing a crocheted hat that was obviously covering a lack of hair. Connie told me that she had just started her second round of chemo. She'd had breast cancer 4 years before, and she'd had a double mastectomy. The day after Christmas, she found out that the cancer had spread to her liver, breastbone, and lungs. She was married, with two small boys, and she'd quit her job because she was exhausted all the time. My heart just broke for her. I knew instantly that she was the one. When she told me that she was a Mary Kay consultant, I was even more certain of my decision because I am one, too.

I went home and wrapped up the multicolored shawl I'd made, printed out a poem and tag to include with the shawl, found Connie's address on the Internet, and promptly drove to her house with a friend. I felt a little odd going to a stranger's house and giving her a shawl, but she was very thankful and overwhelmed. I know it went to the right person. It's amazing how God put Connie in my path and made this decision so clear to me. Now I make as many shawls as I can, and I don't worry about who they will go to.

LAURA ADAMS, Lawrenceville, Georgia

T HIS PATTERN IS SIMPLE ENOUGH FOR MEDITA-
tive knitting, yet interesting enough to keep your attention.
Although lovely as is, the shawl takes on a fun and festive look when a colorful
ribbon yarn is woven across the body of work at regular intervals. To change the
look, try knitting this shawl with different colored yarn. You can also change the type of yarn,
adding more texture. For a multi-colored shawl, experiment by working the K10 rows in black or
cream, adding color to the sections in between. This would be a great way to use up your stash of
yarn for a one-of-a-kind shawl.

FROM
Donna Buse
Grantville, Pennsylvania

RIBBON-TRIMMED SHAWL

Skill Level
Easy

Finished Measurements
56 in long and 21 (23) in wide

Yarn
- Approx 900 yd worsted weight yarn
- Approx 60 yd bulky weight ribbon yarn
- Shown in Red Heart Soft Yarn
  (100% acrylic; 256 yd/5 oz), 4 skeins
  #9114 Honey; Moda Dea Ticker Tape
  (100% nylon; 67 yd/1.75 oz), 1 ball
  #9273 Sunset

Needles
- Size 11 straight or circular needles (or size needed to obtain gauge)

Notions
- Safety pin

Gauge
- 12 sts and 20 rows = 4 in worked in Garter Stitch

RIBBON-TRIMMED SHAWL

DIRECTIONS

Note: Once pattern is established, attach a safety pin to RS of shawl to help keep track of RS and WS rows.

CO 57 (63) sts.

Knit 10 rows.

Next Row (WS):
K3, p3, repeat across.

Next Row (RS):
Knit across.

Repeat last 2 rows for a total of 10 rows.

Repeat these 20 rows until shawl measures 56 in, or desired length, ending with knit 10 rows. BO all sts.

FINISHING

Weave ribbon yarn across body of shawl at pattern changes, as shown in the photo at on p. 136, as follows: Leaving a 12-in end, tie ribbon yarn to edge of shawl at first pattern change. Weave yarn in and out of shawl every few sts. At opposite side of shawl, tie yarn to secure and leave a 12-in end.

Add fringe (see pp. 167–168), if desired, using a combination of shawl yarn and ribbon yarn.

The Spirit of Giving

In October 2005, I read an article about the Prayer Shawl Ministry and decided to make a prayer shawl for myself. My yarn just had to be in the red family, so I purchased home-grown and home-sheared wool from Maine that had been dyed a gloriously rich burgundy. I took my knitting project to church, where I knit during our Sunday service. After the service, a fellow knitter, Pat, asked what I was working on. When I told her, she assumed that the shawl was for Joel, a dear fellow congregant who had been recently diagnosed with lung cancer. In that moment, I knew the shawl wasn't mine, but truly belonged to Joel.

Pat went on to say that her passion was knitting and that if I needed help, she would add her prayers and knitting to the "lap robe" we were making for Joel. The word spread about our Prayer Shawl Ministry, and another volunteer, Dot, took over from Pat. We finished the lap robe and gave it to Joel on Christmas Day 2005. The cancer that doctors predicted would take his life in 6 months gave him 2 years instead, and Joel told everyone that he was still alive because of God, through the prayers and hands of the knitters at Fairfield Grace United Methodist Church. When he passed away in the summer of 2007, the prayer shawl, along with a photo of Joel receiving it, lay atop his coffin.

That was our first shawl. We have since knit and given away 150 shawls, and this has become Pat's ministry in our church. She can knit one shawl per week, by herself. She has recruited men and women to knit and crochet. She taught half a dozen women to knit at our annual women's retreat. For Make a Difference Day 2007, Marge, another participant in our ministry, has planned training for a group of tween girls who want to help. People are knitting alone, in pairs, and in groups and are sharing all types of gifts to help this ministry grow.

Best of all are the stories that come from the recipients. Their doubts, fears, pains, and anxieties are being diminished because the burdens are divided by all the people who are involved in this ministry. Likewise, their healed spirits and joys are multiplied and expanded when shared with the growing prayer shawl community.

CHRISTINE SPEIGHT
Bridgeport, Connecticut

THE BASKETWEAVE STITCH PATTERN CAN BE done by repeating any number of stitches, and while Barbara Thornton chose three for this design, we received shawls based on other combinations: Lynn Everett of Farmington, Connecticut, used six; Pam Wright of Wilmington, Delaware, chose five. Seven symbolized completion in Marian McKittrick's shawl, from Versailles, Indiana. And Barbara Emerson, of Dedham, Massachusetts, used nine, for the days of devotion in the Catholic faith.

FROM
Barbara Thornton
West Chester, Pennsylvania

BASKETWEAVE SHAWL

Skill Level
Easy

Finished Measurements
54 in long and 20 in wide, excluding crocheted border

Yarn
• Approx 700 yd worsted weight yarn
• Shawl shown in Red Heart Super Saver® (100% acrylic; 364 yd/7 oz), 2 skeins #0661 Frosty Green

Needles
• Size 10 straight or circular needles (or size needed to obtain gauge)
• Size I crochet hook

Gauge
• 12 sts and 20 rows = 4 in worked in pattern stitch

DIRECTIONS
CO 63 sts

Rows 1–5: K3, p3 to end.

Rows 6–10: P3, k3 to end.

Repeat Rows 1–10 until shawl measures 54 in, or desired length. BO all sts.

CROCHET BORDER
With crochet hook, attach yarn at right edge of one end of shawl.

Row 1: Working in the CO or BO sts, crochet as follows: Ch 3, sk 2 sts, dc in next st, *ch 2, sk 2 sts, dc in next st, repeat from * across to left edge. After last dc, ch 3, turn.

Row 2: Repeat Row 1, working dc sts in dc sts of previous row. After last dc, cut yarn and pull through last loop. Weave in end.

Repeat Rows 1 and 2 on opposite end of shawl.

Meditation

To some, my shawl looks like a simple basketweave pattern. To me, however, this pattern resembles interlocking links. These links unite me with the Holy Spirit as I pray on each stitch.

The stitches are intertwined, one by one: Father, Son, and Holy Spirit. The knitting changes direction. My left hand works simultaneously with my right hand. The soft tapping sound of the needles is comforting, especially in a group in which all members are knitting quietly together. The soft, tapping sound connects each person in the room to the Holy Spirit—it is silent prayer. The sound reminds me to be thankful for my own life.

My basketweave pattern incorporates the Trinity Stitch, with blocks of three knits and three purls, and the pattern is reversed every five rows. Each stitch, whether knit or purl, is different but the same, interlaced with one another, forming a calming stronghold around the person who will receive it. Every spare minute I have is spent knitting a few rows. God is working through my hands, my mind, and my spiritual self.

Finished. Mmmm, peace. I can hardly wait to start creating the next one, beginning with a single strand, spending precious time in silence, and ending with a shroud of peace and consolation.

BARBARA THORNTON
West Chester, Pennsylvania

MAY THIS SHAWL

May this prayer shawl, made for you with love,
be a mantle and sign of God's healing presence.
May it warm you when you are weary.
May it surround you with ease
in your suffering.
May it encircle you with caring
when you are in pain.
May it comfort you when you feel alone.
May it remind you of God's abiding love.

—RITA ATKINSON
EDMONTON, ALBERTA

FROM
Ann Pettit
Pacific Grove, California

G IVING A SHAWL TO SOMEONE WHO IS GRIEVING can be a daunting experience. Not knowing what the recipient's reaction will be adds pressure to the moment. Thoughts run through your mind: "Is this a good time for her?" "Will he understand what I am giving him?" You know that your gift cannot take away his or her pain. But be assured that a shawl offers a *tangible* gift of unconditional love when words alone cannot express the sympathy, care, and concern you wish to convey. Sometimes, the simple gesture of placing a shawl around someone's shoulders and reciting a few words of a prayer or thought can mean so much. By doing so, you are letting the recipient know that you are thinking of her and that you wish her the best.

This shawl turns the most ordinary of yarns into a soft, cushy fabric particularly suited to embracing one who is grieving. After a bit of practice, you'll find this pattern offers pleasant, easy knitting that goes fast.

LACY SHAWL

Skill Level
Intermediate

Finished Measurements
56 in long and 23 in wide

Yarn
- Approx 800 yd worsted weight yarn
- Shawl shown in Caron Simply Soft (100% acrylic; 366 yd/7 oz), 3 skeins #9907 Grey Heather

Needles
- Size 11 straight or circular needles (or size needed to obtain gauge)

Gauge
- 12 sts and 20 rows = 4 in worked in Stockinette Stitch

LACY SHAWL

DIRECTIONS

CO 64 sts.

Note: When doing either a k2tog or a p2tog, throw yarn *under* needle tip. This makes your sts sit on your needles in a convenient presentation for each following row.

Row 1: K1, *yo, k2tog, repeat from * until 1 st remains, k1.

Row 2: P1, *yo, p2tog, repeat from * until 1 st remains, p1.

Repeat Rows 1 and 2 for about 6 in, ending after completing Row 1.

At this point you can change yarn colors if you desire.

Next Row: Purl across.

Next Row: Knit across.

Repeat these 2 rows once more.

Repeat this pattern sequence, beginning with Row 2, until shawl measures 60 to 70 in, or desired length, ending with 6 in of Rows 1 and 2. BO very loosely.

CINQUAIN

Shawl
heartfelt gift
warming embracing comforting
rest within its softness

—ALICE WANSOR
MELVILLE, NEW YORK

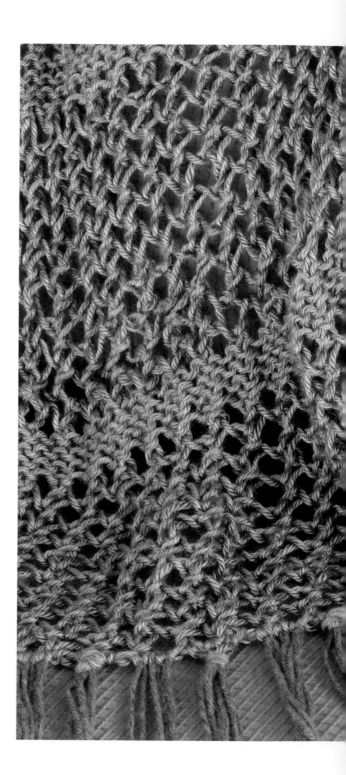

Ask Me

For many years, I searched for my own niche at Lord of Life Lutheran Church. I tried playing in the bell choir, doing new-member orientations, serving in the coffee room, and working with the sacristy team, but none of them seemed to fit. I felt I was not spiritually contributing to the church that had given me so much, and I wondered just how could I make a difference.

One day, out of the blue, I got a craft catalog in the mail. As I flipped through it, I found a page titled "Prayer Shawls" almost at the very end. With great excitement, I thought: "I can knit. I can teach others. I can head up this new ministry." I had found my niche!

I knitted a name tag to wear at church that read, "Ask me," and set out to recruit members. In less than a month we had our first organizational meeting, and 17 people attended. First, we set meeting dates, and then came the decision on where to send our shawls.

I was immediately drawn to a young parishioner named Sarah who had just graduated from college and had entered the Peace Corps. She had been assigned to Armenia. Her mother had joined our Prayer Shawl Ministry, and we asked her if Sarah could use any shawls. Sarah wrote back to us saying that indeed she could. The school where she was teaching had no central heating system, and it was getting very cold. That's all we needed to hear. She asked for 40 shawls, and we got busy. They were blessed in a simple ceremony at church and sent on their way. In the first shipment, we sent 24 shawls to her; every color, shape, and size was produced.

Now, on the eve of sending our second shipment to Sarah to finish "Project Armenia," I feel blessed to be involved with this ministry. It has given me countless hours to think about an unfamiliar country and develop feelings for the people who live there. And I have become closer to church acquaintances, friends, and God. Ask me if a shawl provides comfort. Ask me about 20 fellow church members who have discovered how rewarding it is to be a disciple for Christ with yarn and needles. Ask me if we made a difference in the lives of 40 people in Armenia. Ask me.

SANDY TROUTMAN, Hilliard, Ohio

"POCKET" PRAYER SHAWLS—SMALL RECTANGLES with a tassel at one end—can be carried in pockets or used in situations in which a large shawl is not appropriate or allowed, such as intensive care units of hospitals. Janice Schulz, founder of the Prayer Shawl Ministry at Christ Evangelical Lutheran Church in Heath, Ohio, designed these tiny shawls. In her shawl ministry, a pocket shawl is included whenever a prayer shawl is presented to someone, and one is often given to each member of a family dealing with a major illness or death. The pattern is simple and is a wonderful use of the leftover yarn from making a large shawl.

Prayer cloths, according to Tish Hoar of Mount Vernon, Ohio, can be used to comfort the sick or to mark special occasions. Smaller prayer cloths can be tucked into purses and even helmets. For more information, go to http://sendingtroopsprayers.bravehost.com.

POCKET PRAYERS

Pocket Shawl

FROM
Janice Shulz
Heath, Ohio

Skill Level
Easy

Finished Measurements
Approx 4 in square

Yarn
• Approx 25 yd worsted weight yarn

Needles
• Size 9 straight needles (or size needed to obtain gauge)

Gauge
• 16 sts and 28 rows = 4 in worked in Garter Stitch

DIRECTIONS
CO 16 sts. Knit every row (Garter Stitch) until piece measures 4 in. BO all sts.

Add tassel (see p. 168), at the center of one end.

FROM
Tish Hoar

Mount Vernon, Ohio

Prayer Cloth

Skill Level
Easy

Finished Measurements
Approx 12 in square

Yarn
• Approx 50 yd worsted weight yarn

Needles
• Size 8 straight needles (or size needed to obtain desired gauge)

Gauge
• 16 sts and 34 rows = 4 in worked in Garter Stitch

Note: Gauge is not crucial.

DIRECTIONS
CO on 4 sts.

Row 1: Knit.

Row 2: K2, inc 1 st in next st, k1.

Row 3: K2, inc 1 st in next st, knit to end of row.

Repeat Row 3 until square measures 12 in along one side.

Next Row: K1, k2tog, knit to end of row.

Repeat this row until 5 sts remain.

Next Row: K2, k2tog, k1.

BO remaining 4 sts.

THIS IS A GREAT PATTERN FOR SHAWL MAKERS wishing to learn the basic lace techniques of yarn over and knit two together. In this pattern—a variation on the Fan and Feather or Old Shale pattern—the combination of the two techniques results in a zigzag effect. In the first row, the yarn overs and decreases create the scalloped lace pattern, followed by a simple purl row and a simple knit row. Beginners may want to keep track of these rows as they go along.

Experiment with the yarn and needle size, if you wish, to get different effects. The very bulky hand-dyed yarn used here resulted in a thick, heavy shawl that we affectionately call "a bear." A worsted weight or slightly bulky yarn would create a lighter, lacier effect with size 11 or 13 needles.

FROM
Alice Beck
Christiana, Pennsylvania

ALICE'S LACE SHAWL

Skill Level
Intermediate

Finished Measurements
70 in long and 23 in wide

Yarn
- Approx 700 yd bulky yarn
- Shawl shown in Decadent Fibers Crème Puff (80% merino wool/20% mohair; 140 yd/8 oz), 5 skeins Red Hot Pepper

Needles
- Size 15 straight or circular needles (or size needed to obtain gauge)

Gauge
- 8 sts and 12 rows = 4 in worked in pattern

DIRECTIONS
CO 56 sts.

Row 1: *K1, k2tog, k4, yo, k1, yo, k4, k2tog twice, k4, yo, k1, yo, k4, k2tog, k1. Repeat from * once.

Row 2: Purl across.

Row 3: Knit across.

Repeat Rows 1–3 until shawl measures 70 in, or desired length. BO all sts.

FINISHING
If desired, add simple tassels to the point of each scallop, using two 18-in strands of yarn per tassel (there will be 5 on one side, 6 on the other). See page 168 for details.

The Healer's Touch

In biblical times, one woman had but to touch the fringe of Jesus' garment to be healed. In troubled times, we need but to touch the fringes of our shawls and feel their blessings. They are a gift to us to help us prepare for our final walk. Followers of Jesus had to keep this faith hidden, so often when others were near they would draw outlines of fish in the sand to let each other know that they loved Jesus.

As I knit my prayer shawls, I like to lay the skeins of yarn on a stool to my left, as soon as the yarn can be pulled from the center without stress. Then a miracle happens. It is mysterious, as if light pushes through the skein's tunnel, and it is even brighter at my end of the skein. I pause and feel the presence of God as the yarn works through my hands and becomes a special prayer shawl for someone in need. The glory of God shines round about us and with the ones who receive and use their shawls.

I tell my friends who have received shawls because they are sick, or about to be married, or bereaved, or even in the process of selling a home and moving to an apartment to use the shawl in special quiet time. Praising God, giving thanks, even letting Jesus know your thoughts are ways of answering Jesus' call.

RUTH BEITELSPACHER
Aberdeen, South Dakota

A GLIMPSE OF HEAVEN

Our prayer shawls can be an aid to praying
as a cane is an aid for the lame.
They are like a hug from God,
our Heavenly Father.
These shawls touch Heaven to earth.
The warmth we feel is like a glimpse of what
being in Heaven would be like.
The glory of the Lord shines round about
you as you wrap it around you.
Our faith is strengthened as we pray more
often in this comfort.

—RUTH BEITELSPACHER
ABERDEEN, SOUTH DAKOTA

PRAYER SHAWL
FOR LILY

THIS GRACEFUL AND DELICATE SHAWL IS PERFECT FOR a very special person on your shawl-knitting list. The light mohair/silk yarn makes a warm, enveloping shawl that is incredibly light and airy at the same time.

Skill Level
Experienced

Finished Measurements
73½ in long and 22 in wide

Yarn
- Approx 690 yd of lightweight mohair or mohair-blend yarn
- Shawl shown in Rowan Kidsilk Haze (70% kid mohair/30% silk; 229 yd/0.875 oz), 3 balls #582 Trance
- Smooth waste yarn in a contrasting color

Needles
- Size 7 straight needles (or size needed to obtain gauge)
- Two size 6 double-pointed needles

Notions
- Stitch holders
- Stitch markers
- Approx 285 seed beads
- Tapestry needle

Gauge
- 20 sts and 24 rows = 4 in worked in Snowdrop Stitch, after blocking. Please check carefully.

JEAN MOSS'S

PRAYER SHAWL FOR LILY

SNOWDROP STITCH

For center panel of shawl; multiple of 8 + 3.

Sl first st and k1b last st on every row. There is an allowance for this in pattern repeat—that is, there are 2 selvedge sts. This creates an edge with which to attach knit-on border.

Rows 1 and 3: *M1 (wrap yarn around needle to make 1 st), sl 1 st purlwise, k2tog, psso, m1, k5; rep from * to last 3 sts, m1, sl 1, k2tog, psso, m1.

Rows 2, 4, 6, and 8: Purl.

Row 5: *K3, m1, sl 1, k1, psso, k1, k2tog, m1; rep from * to last 3 sts, k3.

Row 7: *M1, sl 1, k2tog, psso, m1, k1; rep from * to last 3 sts, m1, slip 1, k2tog, psso, m1.

Repeat these 8 rows.

QUEEN'S LACE EDGING

For edging.

CO 12 sts.

Row 1: K4, yo, k2tog, k2, yo, k2tog, yo, k2.

Row 2: K2, yo, k2tog, yo, k5, yo, k2tog, k2.

Row 3: K1, k2tog, yo, k7, yo, k2tog, yo, k2.

Row 4: K2, yo, k2tog, yo, k6, k2tog, yo, k3.

Row 5: K4, yo, k2tog, k3, k2tog, yo, k1, yo, k2tog, yo, k2.

Row 6: K2, yo, k2tog, yo, k3, yo, k2tog, k4, yo, k2tog, k2.

Row 7: K1, k2tog, yo, k4, k2tog, yo, k5, yo, k2tog, yo, k2.

Row 8: K2, yo, k2tog, yo, k1, yo, k2tog, k1, k2tog, yo, k4, k2tog, yo, k3.

Row 9: K4, yo, k2tog, k4, yo, k3tog, yo, k3, yo, k2tog, yo, k2.

Row 10: CO 2, bring up 5 beads, BO 2, k2 (1 will already have been knitted after BO), yo, k2tog, yo, k5, yo, k2tog, k6, yo, k2tog, k2.

Row 11: K1, k2tog, yo, k6, k2tog, yo, k1, yo, k2tog, k1, k2tog, (yo, k2tog) twice, k1.

Row 12: K1, k2tog, yo, k2tog, yo, k3tog, yo, k3, yo, k2tog, k3, k2tog, yo, k3.

Row 13: K4, yo, k2tog, k1, k2tog, yo, k4, k2tog, (yo, k2tog) twice, k1.

Row 14: K1, k2tog, (yo, k2tog) twice, k1, k2tog, yo, k5, yo, k2tog, k2.

Row 15: K1, k2tog, yo, k7, yo, k3tog, (yo, k2tog) twice, k1.

Row 16: K1, k2tog, (yo, k2tog) twice, k5, k2tog, yo, k3.

Row 17: K4, yo, k2tog, k3, k2tog, (yo, k2tog) twice, k1.

Row 18: K1, k2tog, (yo, k2tog) twice, k4, yo, k2tog, k2.

Row 19: K1, k2tog, yo, k4, k2tog, (yo, k2tog) twice, k1.

Row 20: K1, k2tog, (yo, k2tog) twice, k1, k2tog, yo, k3.

Repeat Rows 1–20.

CENTER PANEL

Using straight needles and a Cable Cast On (see p. 167), CO on 69 sts and work Setup Row for Snowdrop Stitch pattern as follows, placing markers on 9th and every subsequent 8th st across row:

Set-Up Row:

Sl 1, *m1 (wrap yarn around needle to make 1 st), sl 1 st purlwise, k2tog, psso, m1, k5; repeat from * slipping markers to last 4 sts, m1, sl 1, k2tog, psso, m1, k1-b. **Note:** First and last sts are always selvedge sts.)

Work Rows 1–8 of Snowdrop Stitch pattern 50 times, then cut yarn and place sts on holder.

EDGING

Thread beads onto yarn. Using double-pointed needles and a

smooth waste yarn in a contrasting color, CO 12 sts and work 4 rows in Stockinette Stitch. Break waste yarn, change to shawl yarn, and work Queen's Lace Edging, starting on fifth hole from bottom up left side of center panel. Knit on edging as you go, attaching it at end of every second row by picking up 1 st and then binding off 1 st into each space (1 space = 2 rows) that forms selvedge edge, matching RS to RS. Work 191 single joins, which brings you to first corner (Corner A).

Notes

Single join: Work once into one selvedge hole (or 1 st along top edge, or 1 ch along CO edge)—2 rows.

Double join: Work twice into one selvedge hole (or 1 st along top edge, or 1 ch along CO edge)—4 rows.

Triple join: Work three times into one selvedge hole (or 1 st along top edge, or 1 ch along CO edge)—6 rows.

Turning Corner A

See drawing on p. 154. Starting 5 spaces from top/bottom of selvedge, work 4 double joins and 1 triple join, turn corner, then work 1 triple join and 3 double joins along CO/BO edge.

Continue around shawl, working a further 60 single joins along the top edge, then work Corner B.

Turning Corner B

See drawing on p. 154. Starting 5 sts from end of BO edge, work 4 double joins, then 1 triple join, turn corner, then work 1 triple join and 3 double joins to next 4 spaces along selvedge.

Continue working a further 191 single joins to the next Corner A and work as before, working into the chains of the CO edge. Work 59 single joins along CO edge and then work the final Corner B as before, starting on the fifth ch from end.

When you have completed this you will have done 58 repeats of Queen's Lace Edging.

Leave sts on knitting needle. Break yarn, leaving a 10-in end. Thread yarn end onto tapestry needle.

FINISHING

Carefully remove waste yarn from beginning of edging and place 12 live sts onto free knitting needle. Using Kitchener Stitch, graft tog start and finish of edging as follows:

Hold two knitting needles parallel and close tog, with yarn coming from right end of back needle and RS of edging facing out.

Step 1: With tapestry needle, bring yarn through first st on front needle as if to knit, and sl st off knitting needle.

Step 2: Bring yarn through second st of front needle as if to purl, and leave st on knitting needle.

Step 3: Bring yarn through first st of back needle as if to purl, and sl st off knitting needle.

Step 4: Bring yarn through second st of back needle as if to knit and leave st on knitting needle.

Repeat Steps 1–4 until all sts are used up. Weave in end and snip off.

THOUGHTS FOR LILY

*May this shawl
light gently on your shoulders
Bringing comfort and peace.*

*Like a snowdrop in January
heralding the promise of spring,
May you feel swaddled
and strengthened,
Valued and cherished.*

*As this shawl
moves through the generations,
May all feel the love and joy
knitted into every stitch
and remember.*

—JANET BRISTOW

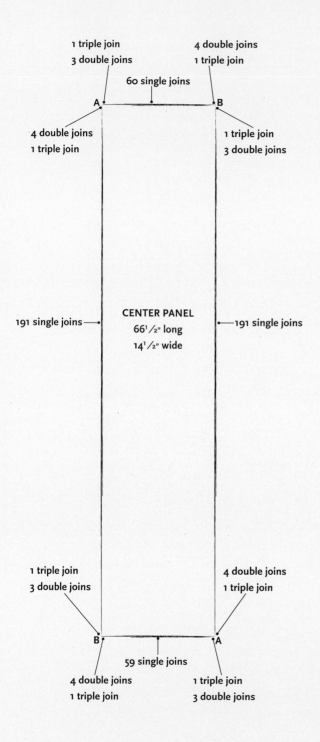

1 triple join
3 double joins

4 double joins
1 triple join

A   60 single joins   B

4 double joins
1 triple join

1 triple join
3 double joins

191 single joins →

CENTER PANEL
66$\frac{1}{2}$" long
14$\frac{1}{2}$" wide

← 191 single joins

1 triple join
3 double joins

4 double joins
1 triple join

B   59 single joins   A

4 double joins
1 triple join

1 triple join
3 double joins

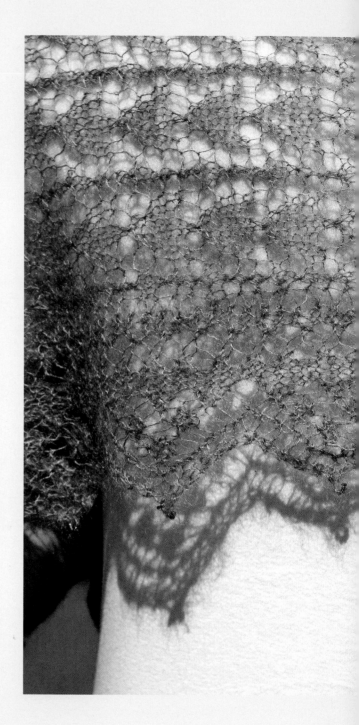

To My Mother

At the beginning of February 2007, my family was celebrating the birth of my first grandchild, Isabella, when my mother, Lily, took a nasty fall. Bedridden, my mother came to stay at our home. Unfortunately, she was so weak all she could do was sleep.

Soon after, I received an e-mail from the Prayer Shawl Ministry asking if I would submit a shawl for this book, and I quickly declined. But over the next few days, despite myself, each time I went into Lily's room, I started to imagine her wrapped in my unknit shawl. Its color would be turquoise, the color of emotional healing, protection, and strength. The yarn would be light as a feather, as she was so bruised she couldn't bear anyone to touch her. The stitches would have to be transparent and open—the shawl cried out for delicate lace.

Gradually, the shawl became something I had to do. Not long after, Lily was admitted to hospital, and, with the extra time, I began to transform the design that existed in my head into reality. My mother's birthday is in January, the darkest time of the year, when only the knife-sharp leaves of the snowdrop dare thrust their silver-green blades through the frozen soil.

Harbingers of spring, these delicate little plants are strong in adversity. I chose snowdrops for the center panel of Lily's shawl in anticipation of many happy and healthy years to come.

My mother's life, like many of her generation, has not been easy and was largely spent working in a Lancashire cotton mill. So for the border, I chose the Queen's Lace Edging in the hope that she'll live every day of the rest of her life in regal fashion. The tiny beads knitted regularly into the edging are a mantra for finding delight in every day. They are small, because some days you have to look extra hard. Lily likes to poke her own fire, as she puts it, but it's difficult to be independent, elderly, and alone. When she wears her shawl, I hope the love that's knitted into it will give her the strength she needs to lead the life she wants and the wisdom to know what that is.

This shawl has been an emotional journey for me. Coming at a time when I felt vulnerable and unsure myself, it helped me find a way of coping. While working on it, I found myself thinking that everything I was wishing for Lily I would wish for Izzi, too. So this shawl is dedicated to both my mother and my little granddaughter in the hope that the love and joy that went into its making will surround them both always.

JEAN MOSS
York and Wales, United Kingdom

FROM
Barbara St. Cyr
West Yarmouth, Massachusetts

THIS SHAWL—THE CAPE COD VERSION OF THE original prayer shawl pattern—came as a result of Barbara St. Cyr's Cape Cod–based Prayer Shawl Ministry misreading the knit three, purl three instructions. Instead of creating the intended Seed Stitch effect, their pattern turned out ribbed—and they liked it that way! It's shown here in a beautiful silk and wool yarn, in a colorway that spoke Cape Cod to us.

There are many ways to finish this shawl. With the yarn used here, a simple fringe (see pp. 167–168) gains a unique texture. The group also adds tassels (see p. 168) on every rib or crochets a scallop shell edging (see "Finishing" in Nursing Shawl pattern p. 99) continuing the Cape Cod theme. Barbara also suggests knitting two 4-in by 5-in pockets to sew on the outside of the shawl. Into these pockets, the Cape Cod ministry places blessed medals, charms, mini-rosaries, prayer cards, notes with blessings from the knitters, or cards explaining the Prayer Shawl Ministry.

CAPE COD SHAWL

Skill Level
Easy

Finished Measurements
65 in long and 18 in wide

Yarn
- Approx 700 yd heavy worsted weight yarn
- Shawl shown in Alchemy Yarns Wabi-Sabi (66% silk/34% wool; 86 yd/1.75 oz), 9 skeins #86C Slip Stream

Needles
- Size 11 straight or circular needles (or size needed to obtain gauge)

Gauge
- 12 sts and 16 rows = 4 in worked in pattern

CAPE COD SHAWL

DIRECTIONS

CO 57 sts.

Row 1: *K3, p3, repeat from * to end of row, end k3.

Row 2: *P3, k3, repeat from * to end of row, end p3. (**Note:** You are knitting the knit sts and purling the purl sts to form a ribbed pattern.)

Repeat Rows 1 and 2 until shawl measures 65 in, or desired length.

Block shawl lightly to flatten ribbing because shawl will draw in considerably.

MAY THIS SHAWL

May this prayer shawl, made for you with love, be a mantle and sign of God's healing presence. May it warm you when you are weary. May it surround you with ease in your suffering. May it encircle you with caring when you are in pain. May it comfort you when you feel alone. May it remind you of God's abiding love.

—PRAYER SHAWL MINISTRY OF
THE GOOD SHEPHERD CATHOLIC
WOMEN'S LEAGUE
EDMONTON, ALBERTA, CANADA

The Texture of Healing

Though I adore all aspects of knitting, I experience a different and more profound enthusiasm when I knit for another person. I love to create something special that I wouldn't likely make for myself. As mothers will do something for their children that they wouldn't dream of doing for themselves, knitters display this quality of selflessness and deepest compassion when knitting for other individuals.

So it goes with the fiber we select when we knit for another. While we may choose a yarn for ourselves that is practical, on sale, or "just good enough"; generosity of the heart comes into play when selecting fiber that is intended for someone else. We look to the extraordinary. We long for something soothing, soft, and remarkable to the senses to communicate our caring, our love, and our gratitude. Knitting for another makes possible a kind of reciprocity of the heart. The texture of healing is offered to both the knitter and the recipient of the gift.

Something truly spiritual happens in this process, and it is particularly noticeable when working with exquisite yarns. The unique qualities of a fiber that is made by hand, with great love and care, are wonderful companions to gift knitting. The inimitable softness and holistic feel of a natural fiber that has not been chemically treated are genuine gifts to the hands of the knitter. The luxuriousness with which a silk or cashmere slides effortlessly through the fingers is a blessing to the one who works in stitch and prayer for another. Beautiful color enriches the experience of the knitter throughout the making of the piece. The *process* of knitting becomes a celebration, a rejoicing for the knitter, and this experience is passed along in the *product* constructed. It makes the experience more than, "I knit this piece and I am giving it to you." Instead, it becomes, "I knit this piece and had a wonderful time when I made it, so I am giving you that joy, as well."

Thus there is a symbiotic relationship between knitter and recipient. The fiber is a conduit and holds alive prayer. It also reminds us that we are worthy of such beauty. Why shouldn't our hands hold fiber that is most satisfying to the touch? Why wouldn't our eyes delight in the splendor of seductive color in each sacred stitch? And why not experience the realm of joy to the fullest, when we knit for another? We choose to knit because we choose to love. Deep healing comes from creative expression. This healing is further enhanced when we give ourselves the pleasure of working with the finest fiber we can find, transforming our creative expression into something lovely we can share.

GINA WILDE
Founder, Alchemy Yarns of Transformation
Sebastopol, California

APPENDICES

HOW TO START A
PRAYER SHAWL
MINISTRY

Forming a Prayer Shawl Ministry is a great way to involve many people in meeting the needs of others, whether in a faith community, hospice, hospital, circle of friends, or knitting group. We even know of a yoga group that incorporates shawl making into their practice. If you belong to a faith community, meet with clergy and staff to see if the ministry could be introduced there. If you will be bringing this to the community in which you live, find a space that could accommodate your needs, such as a library, community center, senior center, or classroom for continuing adult education. You could also simply gather a friend or two and meet in each other's homes. To invite members into your Prayer Shawl Ministry, consider the following:

• Place an ad in your church's or synagogue's bulletin; your organization's newsletter; your local newspaper; or publications or brochures sent out by community centers, libraries, senior centers, and continuing adult education offices.

• Make a flyer and/or sign-up sheet to post on bulletin boards at various locations, such as those just listed. If appropriate— for example, at the meeting place of your faith community—have a shawl on display.

• Strive to be as inclusive as possible in your search for group members— extending the invitation to knitters in faith communities different from your own opens the door for interfaith dialogue and better understanding of different beliefs and cultures.

• Visit www.shawlministry.com and use the downloadable brochure as a handout to give to those interested in joining your group. Customize the brochure with your own meeting location, date, time, and contact information.

• Schedule a Prayer Shawl Ministry Workshop by contacting us at shawlministry@yahoo.com to the attention of Janet. For further information, see the workshop page on the Prayer Shawl Ministry website for details.

At your first meeting, you will want to do the following:

• Decide how often you will meet—weekly, semimonthly, or monthly—and finalize a time.

• Have a brainstorming session, discussing the style or format of your Prayer Shawl Ministry meetings and who the prayer shawl recipients will be. Will you be offering the shawls to the members of your faith community; to local hospitals, hospices, and shelters; or to a charity? Get suggestions from clergy, your pastoral care team, social workers, parish nurses, or other members of your community. Remember that while you often will know who a shawl is for, sometimes you won't.

• It's good to have a number of shawls on hand that are available to the staff and visitors of someone in need in a hospital, nursing home, or private home. If you'll be supplying shawls to a shelter, hospital, or oncology center on a regular basis, inquire about the approximate number of shawls that will be required. Decide if you will be able to meet those needs. If not, consider joining with other Prayer Shawl Ministry groups to supply the shawls.

• Decide on a method for recording to whom the shawls are given and on what date. Because of privacy issues, it isn't necessary to record the last name of a recipient; a last initial will do. Or you can simply describe the recipient—for example, "a woman undergoing mastectomy" or "a man having heart surgery."

Finally, although this is a ministry of the heart and based on prayer, there are some very nuts-and-bolts issues to address, as well. Although the following probably don't have to be decided during the first meeting, you'll want your group to find answers to these questions, too:

• How will the yarn and other supplies be acquired? Will you have a yarn drive? Ask for donations? Will you accept unused yarn from knitters' stashes or only newly purchased yarn?

• If you plan to purchase yarn, where will the money come from? Can you ask for donations from your faith community or other groups? If donations are given, to whom is the check made out?

• If you purchase yarn, who will buy it and where will it be stored?

• How will the shawls be packaged, and who will do that? Will you include a standard note of explanation with each shawl? Will there be a standard prayer or blessing attached?

• Where will the finished shawls be kept? Who will have access to them?

• Will the shawls be blessed before delivery, and if so, how?

• Will the shawls be given to members of your faith community or organization only? If so, who will deliver them, and how will the shawls be presented?

• Will the shawls be given to people from outside groups, such as shelters, hospices, and hospitals? If so, how often will they be delivered and who will do it?

Because this is a prayerful process, remember to begin each gathering, planning meeting, or ministry circle with some type of ritual, prayer, or blessing. Encourage participants to write their own prayers or write a group prayer that will be included with each shawl given. Some groups begin their gatherings by reading a selection from an inspirational book or scripture and sharing their thoughts on it as they knit.

Every now and then, it's nice to pass someone's shawl-in-progress around the circle. Members can choose to add a few stitches or rows of their own or just hold it quietly, perhaps adding a blessing or wish for the recipient. At the end of your time together, invite members to gather around all the shawls, finished and unfinished, place a hand on them, and recite in unison a prayer or blessing.

As you continue to come together to share thoughts and insights, it will become clearer what direction your particular group will take. Remain open to Divine guidance and don't worry about to whom the shawls will go. The recipients will come to you with ease. Best of all, notice the blessings that flow between the knitter and the recipient and around your faith community, your circle, and your lives.

KNITTING ABBREVIATIONS

approx	approximate(ly)
BO	bind off
CC	contrasting color
ch	chain (crochet)
CO	cast on
dc	double crochet
dec	decrease
k	knit
k1-b	knit 1 stitch through the back loop
kf&b	knit in the front and back of 1 stitch (increase)
k2tog	knit 2 stitches together
in	inch(es)
inc	increase
MC	main color
m1	make 1 stitch (increase)
oz	ounce(s)

p	purl
psso	pass slipped stitch over decrease)
p2tog	purl 2 stitches together (decrease)
RS	right side
sc	single crochet
sk	skip (crochet)
sl	slip
ssk	slip 1 stitch knitwise, slip 1 stitch knitwise, knit the 2 slipped stitches together (decrease)
st/sts	stitch/stitches
tog	together
WS	wrong side
yd	yard(s)
yo	yarn over

STANDARD YARN WEIGHTS

ACTUAL YARN	NUMBERED BALL	DESCRIPTION	STS/4 IN	NEEDLE SIZE
Superfine	1	Sock, baby, fingering	27–32	27–32 2.25–3.25 mm (U.S. 1–3)
Fine	2	Sport, baby	23–26	3.25–3.75 mm (U.S. 3–5)
Light	3	DK, light worsted	21–24	3.75–4.5 mm (U.S. 5–7)
Medium	4	Worsted, afghan, Aran	16–20	4.5–5.5 mm (U.S. 7–9)
Bulky	5	Chunky, craft, rug	12–15	5.5–8.0 mm (U.S. 9–11)
Super bulky	6	Bulky, roving	6–11	8 mm and larger (U.S. 11 and larger)

COLOR & SYMBOLOGY

This color chart, while not authoritative, is a blending from the different sources we've explored through the years. We invite you to use it as a starting point and guideline to begin the prayerful process of shawl making.

COLOR CHART

Red—love, passion, respect, energy, enthusiasm, courage, vigor, health, understanding

Pink—friendship, compassion, sensitivity, generosity, soothing, warm-heartedness, gratitude

Orange—thoughtfulness, vitality, creativity

Yellow—wisdom, learning, optimism, intuition, faith, well-being, friendship, energy, happiness, sociability, joy, gladness, goodness

Green—earth, healing, prosperity, fertility, clarity, sympathy, hope, renewal, health, confidence, abundance, growth, life, permanence, peace, relaxation, spring

Aqua—courage, balance, harmony, stability

Blue—water, healing, meditation, intuition, peace, tranquility, honesty, loyalty, communication, sincerity, wisdom, spirituality, eternity, self-esteem, universal color, coolness, calmness, unity

Indigo—wisdom, insight, instinct, spiritual nature

Violet—spirit, spirituality, intuition, truth, memory, nostalgia, humility, comfort during grief or mourning, peace

Purple—power, leadership, royalty, truth, justice, temperance, spirituality, wisdom

Brown—wholesomeness, honesty, steadfastness, simplicity, friendliness, dependability, practical, down-to-earth, warmth

Beige/Tan—optimism, simplicity, calmness

Black—self-confidence, strength, absorbs negativity, mature wisdom, harmony

White—spirit, light, air, innocence, protection, peace, purity, gentleness, perfection, holiness, maidenhood, illumination, reverence, humility, winter

Gold—masculine energy, enlightenment, sacred, durable

Silver—feminine energy, flexibility

Gray—strength, balance, wisdom

SYMBOLISM OF NUMBERS

As you create your own prayer shawl designs, add tassels, or knit the patterns in this book, remember that all numbers have meanings and can be objects of meditation or symbolic significance.

0—transformation and change, wholeness, the world, new beginnings. In Islam, it is the number of Divine Essence; in the Jewish tradition, limitless light. This can be symbolized in a shawl by not adding fringe.

1—the universe, God, Goddess, single-hood, new life, solitude, prayer

2—balance, union, unity, marriage, commitment, purification, hospitality, wisdom, insight. It also symbolizes yin/yang, parent/child, and the two greatest Commandments: (1) Love God with your heart, mind, and soul, and (2) Love your neighbor as yourself.

3—Father, Son, and Holy Spirit; faith, hope, and love; earth; earth, sky, and sea; thought, word, and deed; in Hinduism, creation, destruction, and preservation; in Japanese culture, the Three Treasures: truth, courage, and compassion

4—generosity, home, the seasons, the lunar phases, the four stages of a butterfly (larva, caterpillar, chrysalis, and butterfly). It also represents the four apostles in the Christian tradition (Matthew, Mark, Luke, and John) and the four mysteries of Catholicism (joyful, luminous, sorrowful, and glorious).

5—power, strength, star, wishes, the human body (think of Leonardo da Vinci's Vitruvian Man); the Five Pillars of Islam (declaration of faith, prayer, fasting, giving alms, and pilgrimage to Mecca); the five wounds of Christ

6—six senses, six days of creation; in Catholicism, the Six Perfections (concentration, effort, ethical behavior, generosity, patience, wisdom)

7—good luck, seven chakras, seven notes on a music scale, seven days in a week; in China, the seven stages of a woman's life; in Catholicism, the Seven Contrary Virtues (humility, kindness, abstinence, chastity, patience, liberality, diligence)

8—luck, enlightenment, intellect, eight petals of the lotus; in Islam, the eight paradises; in China, the eight stages of a man's life; in Christianity, the eight beatitudes

9—unconsciousness

10—reality; the Ten Commandments

SYMBOLISM
Sewn onto a shawl or tied into the fringe, charms, beads, and gemstones add decoration and still more symbolic meaning into a shawl.

SHAPES
Circle—marriage, beginning, eternity

Triangle—trinity, woman, creative intellect

Spiral—journey, feminine wisdom, transformation, introspection

Heart—love, unity, friendship

Square—balance, completion

RELIGIOUS SYMBOLS
Cross—Christianity, sacrifice, salvation, creation, redemption

Star of David—Judaism

Yin/Yang—balance, dualism

Wheel—universe, progress

Claddagh—loyalty, friendship, romantic love

Pentacle—Wiccan symbol of integration of body and spirit

Dreamcatcher—Ojibwa (Chippewa) symbol of protection; traps negative spirits

STITCH DEFINITIONS & SPECIAL TECHNIQUES

KNITTING STITCHES

Slip
Pass a stitch from one needle to the next without working it.

Yarn Over
Wrap the yarn around the right needle as if you were knitting a stitch but do not work a new stitch (increase 1 stitch). On the next row, knit or purl into this loop as you would any other stitch.

Knit into the Front and Back (Kf&b)
Knit into a stitch as usual, but leave it on the left needle. Bring the tip of the right needle around to the back, knit into the back loop of the same stitch, and slip it off the needle (increase 1 stitch).

Make 1 Stitch (m1)
With the tip of the left needle inserted from front to back, lift the horizontal strand between stitches onto the left needle; knit this strand through the back loop (increase 1 stitch).

Pass Slipped Stitch Over (PSSO)
Slip the first stitch knitwise, knit the next stitch, pass the slipped stitch over the knit one and off the needle (decrease 1 stitch).

Slip, Slip, Knit (SSK)
Working as if to knit, slip the next 2 stitches, one at a time, to the right needle. Insert the left needle into the front loops of the 2 slipped stitches (from left to right). Knit the 2 slipped stitches together, wrapping the yarn in the usual way (decrease 1 stitch).

I-Cord
Using double-pointed needles, cast on the required number of stitches (usually 4 or 5); the working yarn will be on the left side of the needle. *Hold the needle with the stitches in your left hand, bring the yarn around behind the stitches to the right side and knit the stitches from right to left, pulling the yarn tightly behind the work when knitting the first stitch. Do not turn. Repeat from * until the cord is the desired length.

Stockinette Stitch
Knit the RS rows and purl the WS rows.

Garter Stitch
Knit all rows.

Seed Stitch
Knit 1, purl 1 across the row. For all subsequent rows, knit the purl stitches and purl the knit stitches as they face you.

Kitchener Stitch

The stitches to be joined together are on two needles, held parallel and close together with the yarn coming from the right end of the back needle. Break the yarn, leaving a 10-in end (depending on how many stitches will be grafted together). Thread the yarn end onto a tapestry needle.

• Bring the yarn through the first stitch on the front needle as if to knit, and slip the stitch off the knitting needle.

• Bring the yarn through the second stitch on the front needle as if to purl, and leave the stitch on the knitting needle.

• Bring the yarn through the first stitch on the back needle as if to purl, and slip the stitch off the knitting needle.

• Bring the yarn through the second stitch on the back needle as if to knit and leave it on the knitting needle.

Repeat these steps until all the stitches are used up. Weave in the end and snip off.

CROCHET STITCH
Reverse Single Crochet

Working from left to right, insert the hook into the next stitch, yarn over and pull up a loop, yarn over and pull it through both loops on the hook.

CASTING ON AND BINDING OFF
Cable Cast On

To work a cable cast on: Make a slip knot on left needle (Figure 1). Working into this knot's loop, knit a stitch and place it on left needle (Figure 2). Insert right needle between last two stitches (Figure 3). From this position, knit a stitch and place it on left

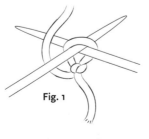

Fig. 1

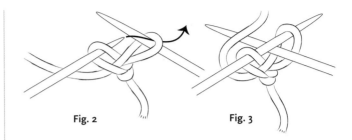

Fig. 2   Fig. 3

needle. Repeat step 3 for each additional stitch.

Knitted Cast On

Knit 1 stitch without removing the original stitch from the left needle. Transfer the new stitch back on to the left needle by slipping it knitwise. Continue in this manner, always making the new stitch into the one just transferred to the left needle.

Bind Off Together (BO tog)

This is a method for binding off stitches and, at the same time, joining them to a cast-on edge. With a separate needle, pick up the same number of stitches along the cast-on edge that you will be binding off. Hold the binding-off and cast-on stitches side by side with right sides together and both needles pointing in the same direction. Slip a third needle into the first stitch on both needles and knit them together. Knit the second stitch in the same manner, then pass the first stitch over the second, binding off 1 stitch. Repeat across all stitches.

FRINGES AND EDGE TREATMENTS
Fringe

Cut yarn to the length specified in pattern, or twice the length of desired fringe (for example, cut 16-in lengths for an 8-in fringe). Holding together as many lengths as desired, fold the lengths in half, insert a crochet hook into the first stitch on either the cast-on or bound-off edge of the shawl, pull up a loop by catching the lengths of fringe at their center point and pulling the loose ends through the loop. Pull to tighten. Repeat across the edge. Trim the fringe even, if necessary.

Macramé Fringe

For a macramé look, repeat rows of double-knot fringe until desired effect is achieved.

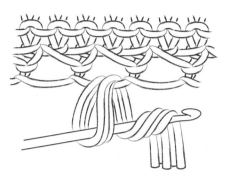

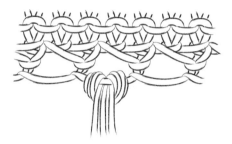

Double-Knot Fringe

Follow the directions given under "Fringe." After completing the fringe, turn the shawl so the right side of the work is facing you. Work knots as shown in the diagram below.

Tassel

Wrap yarn around an object (piece of cardboard, pack of cards) the same length as desired length of tassel. When finished, thread a length of yarn on a needle and slide it under the top wraps of the tassel. Tie tightly, and do not trim (use the strands to attach the tassel to the project). Slide a scissors blade under the bottom wraps and cut. Tie a second length of yarn around the tassel about $1/2$ in from the top and tie tightly. Trim the ends to tassel length.

Pompom

Cut 2 cardboard circles the diameter of the desired pompom. Cut a 1-in-diameter hole out of the middle of both circles. Cut a small wedge out of both, then hold the circles together with these openings aligned. Wrap yarn tightly all the way around both circles. When finished, slide a scissors blade between the two circles and cut the yarn around the outer edge. Wrap a length of yarn around the strands between the circles and tie tightly. Slip the circles off the completed pompom and trim the pompom evenly, leaving the tie intact to sew onto the project.

DESIGNERS

Kristin Spurkland is the author of *Knits from the Heart*; *Crochet from the Heart*; *Blankets, Hats, and Booties*; and *The Knitting Man(ual)*. When not knitting, among other things, she volunteers at the House of Dreams cat shelter. For more, visit her website www.kristinspurkland.com.

Jodi Lewanda a textile design graduate from New York City's Fashion Institute of Technology, and has had her work published by JCA/Reynolds, Nashua Handknits, Lion Brand, and Classic Elite. Her work can also be seen in magazines such as *Knit It!* and *Cast On*.

Trudy Van Stralen, a founder of Louet and a longtime knitter, designs patterns and new yarns for Louet, North America, which is known for its high-quality knitting, spinning, and weaving products, ranging from innovative spinning wheels to beautiful yarns crafted from materials such as Merino wool, linen, and kid mohair. For more go to www.louet.com.

Kaffe Fassett's love of color, pattern, and texture is nowhere more apparent than in his designs for knitting, needlepoint, and quilting. A best-selling author and much-beloved knitting designer, he has hosted his own TV series, *Glorious Colour*, and was the first living textile artist ever to do a one-man exhibition at the Victoria and Albert Museum in London.

Marilyn Webster has knit throughout her life, and her passion for fiber arts includes weaving, spinning, and textile traditions around the world. A former designer for Alchemy Yarns of Transformation, Marilyn has always altered patterns and created her own designs.

Wren Ross is an actor, singer, writer, and devoted knitwear designer. Her cabaret performance "Singing with Every Fiber!" and her CD *Wren's Greatest Knits!* celebrate the delights and dilemmas of crafting with yarn. Wren has also co-authored a book with Daena Giardella called *Changing Patterns: Discovering the Fabric of Your Creativity*. For more information, visit www.wrenross.com.

Kathleen Taylor is a writer, wife, mother, grandma, and lifelong knitter. She has written three knitting books—*Knit One, Felt Too*; *Yarns to Dye For*; and *I ♥ Felt*—and designed sock and sweater patterns for the Knit Picks yarn company. She can be reached at KathisDakotaDreams@blogspot.com.

Melissa Matthay, known for her sense of flair, has been designing knits for more than 25 years. She is regularly commissioned by top international yarn manufacturers and has written many books, among them *The Little Box of Scarves*, *Knits Three Ways*, and her latest, *Kritter Knits*. Learn more about Melissa at www.bymelissa.net.

Nicky Epstein is a well-known knitting designer and prolific author. She is especially famous for her flair for embellishment, attention to detail, and innovative approaches, all reflected in her many books, including *Knitting Never Felt Better*, *Knitting on the Edge*, *Knitting over the Edge*, *Knitting beyond the Edge*, *Knitted Embellishments*, and *Knits for Barbie Doll*.

Carri Hammett is the owner of Coldwater Collaborative, a yarn shop in Minnesota, filled with fine yarns from around the world. She is also the author of *Scarves and Shawls for Yarn Lovers* and *Ready, Set, Knit Cables*. To learn more about Carri and her shop, visit www.coldwateryarn.com.

Brandon Mably designs knitwear patterns for Rowan Yarns and leads workshops on knitwear design and color use throughout the world. For more than a decade, he has been the manager of the Kaffe Fassett Studio in London. Brandon's style favors bold designs and vibrant colors, as featured in his books *Knitting Color: Design Inspiration from Around the World* and *Brilliant Knits: 25 Contemporary Designs*.

British designer **Jean Moss** is known worldwide for her distinctive knits. Author of books, including *Couture Knits*, *Sculptured Knits*, and *Contemporary Classics*, she has designed for Rowan Yarns as well as Ralph Lauren, Benetton, and Laura Ashley. She is the principal designer for Artesano Yarns (www.artesanoyarns.co.uk). For more visit www.jeanmoss.com.

RESOURCES

Visit the following websites to find more information on and sources for the yarns used in this book.

ALCHEMY YARNS OF TRANSFORMATION
www.alchemyyarns.com

LANE BORGOSESIA
Distributed by Trendsetter Yarns
www.trendsetteryarns.com

BERNAT
www.bernat.com

BERROCO
www.berroco.com

CARON
www.caron.com

COLINETTE YARNS
www.colinette.com
Distributed by Unique Kolours
www.uniquekolours.com

DECADENT FIBERS
www.decadentfibers.com

ELMORE-PISGAH
www.elmore-pisgah.com

HIFA ULLGARN
www.nordicfiberarts.com

JO-ANN SENSATIONS
www.joann.com

LANA GATTO (WOOL GATTO)
Distributed by Needful Yarns
www.needfulyarnsinc.com

LION BRAND YARN
www.lionbrand.com

LOUET NORTH AMERICA
www.louet.com

MISTI INTERNATIONAL
www.mistialpaca.com

MODA DEA
www.modadea.com

MOUNTAIN COLORS
www.mountaincolors.com

NASHUA HANDKNITS
www.nashuaknits.com
Distributed by Westminster Fibers
www.westminsterfibers.com

PATONS
www.patonsyarns.com

PLYMOUTH YARN COMPANY INC.
www.plymouthyarn.com

RED HEART
www.coatsandclark.com

ROWAN
www.knitrowan.com
Distributed by Westminster Fibers
www.westminsterfibers.com

SUBLIME
Distributed by Knitting Fever
www.knittingfever.com

TLC
www.coatsandclark.com

INDEX